Epic
INDOOR PIZZA OVEN
COOKBOOK

Recipes and Techniques for All Kinds of Pizza

JONATHON SCHUHRKE

HARVARD
COMMON
PRESS

Quarto.com

© 2025 Quarto Publishing Group USA Inc.
Text © 2025 Santa Barbara Baker LLC
Photography © 2025 Forty North Studio inc.

First Published in 2025 by The Harvard Common Press,
an imprint of The Quarto Group, 100 Cummings Center,
Suite 265-D,
Beverly, MA 01915, USA.
T (978) 282-9590
F (978) 283-2742

The Harvard Common Press titles are also available at dis-
count for retail, wholesale, promotional, and bulk purchase.
For details, contact the Special Sales Manager by email at
specialsales@quarto.com or by mail at The Quarto Group,
Attn: Special Sales Manager, 100 Cummings Center,
Suite 265-D, Beverly, MA 01915, USA.

29 28 27 26 25   1 2 3 4 5

ISBN: 978-0-7603-9321-5

Digital edition published in 2025
eISBN: 978-0-7603-9322-2

Library of Congress Cataloging-in-Publication Data

Names: Schuhrke, Jonathon, author.
Title: Epic indoor pizza oven cookbook : recipes and
techniques for all kinds of pizza / Jonathon Schuhrke.
Identifiers: LCCN 2024031026 | ISBN 9780760393215
(paperback) | ISBN 9780760393222 (ebook)
Subjects: LCSH: Pizza. | LCGFT: Cookbooks.
Classification: LCC TX770.P58 S224 2024 | DDC 641.$^{82}/_{48}$--
dc23/eng/20240715
LC record available at https://lccn.loc.gov/2024031026

Page Layout: Kelley Galbreath
Photography: Andrew Purcell | andrewhughpurcell.com
Styling: Carrie Purcell | carrieannpurcell.com

Printed in China

TO VIOLET

Contents

Introduction
PERFECT PIZZA INDOORS

Indoor pizza ovens have made pizza night, every night, a possibility. From classic, thin-crusted New York-style pizza to cheese-crowned deep-dish, Detroit-style pizza, any type of pizza you can dream of is within reach at home. For this book we head inside for a tour of my favorite styles of pizza to make with an indoor pizza oven.

We hit legendary pizzas, like cracker-thin and crispy Chicago tavern-style pizza with homemade sausage and classic pan pizzas like a butter-crust Sicilian-style square pizza. I even include some niche, regional favorites like New Jersey bar-style pan pizzas in addition to the fun, out-of-the box artisan pizza creations I'm known for.

It's time to unlock epic pizza at home with your indoor pizza oven. Let's go!

In this book you'll learn a variety of doughs and pizza-making techniques all dialed-in for home pizza makers. You'll get the tips and secrets to making pizzeria-quality pizza at home.

THE SECRET INGREDIENT

In pizza, many are looking for secrets to uncover. How could something so simple taste so good, so complex, so soul-satisfying? Often composed of only a few ingredients, but huge on flavor, pizza can seem like magic. In a way, it is; a frothy, bubbling bowl of flour and water turns into a golden brown, crackly crusted, ethereal eating experience. This feels like magic to me.

I'll let you in on something. There is a secret. The best part though: It's often within reach of the home pizza maker. You don't need obscure flours or ancient sourdough starters to make truly epic pizza. What you do need is: time.

In the bustle of a pizzeria time is most often at a premium. When the orders are stacked high and the pizzas makers are in the weeds, pizza making can suddenly become high-stressed. At home, pizza night is a bit more mellow experience. The extra time allows you to get the dough just right and to spend a little more time shaping and topping your pizzas into something you can call epic. Put in the time, and you'll notice the difference.

I encourage you to play around with this variable. Try a same-day pizza dough versus a long, cold-fermented dough and pick up on the differences in flavor and texture as well as any

ease in preparation. From the second the flour hits the water the magic begins, be stoked to be part of it, and go make some epic pizza!

INDOOR PIZZA OVENS

Indoor pizza ovens range from inexpensive, "bare-bones" rigs to more polished indoor pizza-making machines. As long as the oven is able to reach and maintain the temperatures required for baking pizza you should be able to produce epic-level pizza at home.

Far more important than fancy oven settings and aesthetic builds is knowing the dough and how to bake it. With this book I hope to give you that last part. When it comes to indoor oven features, I find the ability to "balance" the heat between the top and bottom heat source in the oven is crucial. Different oven makers refer to this feature by different names and some even allow you to set the balance to specific temperatures instead of the more generic high/low dial. Regardless of how it's implemented the feature makes the entire, diverse world of pizza possible in your home kitchen.

SETTING UP YOUR INDOOR PIZZA OVEN

An indoor pizza oven is best set up in a kitchen area with plenty of room and good ventilation. Even the best oven models can struggle with filtering oven smoke so it's best to be in an area that will allow any excess exhaust to ventilate. When I'm baking a ton of pizzas with an indoor oven, I find that a portable air filter can help clear the air up if needed. Due to the ventilation issues, I don't recommend using indoor pizza ovens for cooking many non-pizza items, save

the oven for pizza and other baked goods. Outdoor pizza ovens are better for this multi-cook functionality.

NO PIZZA OVEN? NO PROBLEM.

While the recipes in this book work best with a dedicated pizza oven, a baking steel in a standard home oven can also be used for most recipes.

INGREDIENTS

Pizza is not the place for disposing of the mystery bag of flour at the back of your cupboard. I try to keep the ingredients in my cookbooks high quality, but easy to source.

FLOUR

With flour, fresh is best. Always make sure your flour isn't past its prime. Old flour will make for off flavors in your dough and it won't rise as well. For my pizza I prefer to use organic flour whenever possible and I mostly stick to easy-to-find brands like King Arthur Baking and Central Milling.

YEAST

The dough recipes were developed using instant dry yeast (IDY). When sold in bulk amounts, Fleischmann's calls this product "Bread Machine" or "rapid rise," it's the same thing as their IDY sold in packets. I find instant dry yeast to produce easy, consistent, and delicious results. If you keep a sourdough starter, experiment with adding a small amount to the recipes for a different dimension of flavor.

TOMATOES

For most pizza sauces, canned tomatoes are the way to go. Canned tomatoes are picked and packed at their prime. The tomato flavor is intense in the best way for pizza. I use a mix of styles of canned tomatoes in the recipes, use the best you can get your hands on. If you're lucky enough to have small, regional brands, give them a try, they're often awesome for pizza. If you make pizza frequently, the larger #10 cans of "ground tomatoes" work well for most pizza applications and can be substituted in the recipes in this book.

CHEESE

Go ahead, go shred. Shredding your own cheese makes for better cheese pulls, and overall, a better melt. I'm throwing an exception in this book. If you want to achieve the high, crispy, lacey edges that have become desirable with Detroit-style pizza, grab the bag.

For fresh mozzarella cheese, if you have access to mozzarella cheese made somewhere fresh, in-house daily, that's what you want. Otherwise look for "fresh" mozzarella that's packed in minimal liquid, it's typically shrink-wrapped, not sold in tubs of water.

MEATS

I try to stick to freshly sliced meats for topping my pizzas. Hit the deli-counter for charcuterie and get it sliced to order at the perfect thickness. My exception is pepperoni, pre-sliced, "cup 'n char" pepperoni just works really well and has that signature flavor that many expect when biting into a pepperoni pie.

VEGETABLES

The farmer's market is where I find my veggie inspirations and the best quality produce for topping pizza. I like to showcase the true flavors of my fresh vegetable ingredients. I find that searching for farm-fresh ingredients is worth it.

PIZZA STYLES

This cookbook is split between pizza styles baked directly on the oven stone and other pizza styles baked in pans. Either way you go the recipes are easy to approach and to achieve pizzeria-quality results at home. Indoor pizza ovens are extremely versatile at recreating a wide range of pizza styles at home. I hope you try them all.

PAN PIZZAS

The pan pizza recipes are best made in pans designed specifically for pizza making but can be made in any similarly sized baking pan. I've designed all the pan pizza recipes for easy proofing directly in the pan. The dough can be stretched and shaped to the pan before the cold proofing, making it as simple as popping the pan out of the fridge in the morning the day you're going to make pizza.

SECRETS FOR STRETCHING

Stretching pizza can feel stressful. It shouldn't, be sure to set yourself up for success.

Pizza dough that's properly proofed and brought to temperature will be easy to work with and produce a beautiful crust. To prevent the dough from sticking to your work surface or pizza peel while you stretch and top the pizza, flour the bottom of the pizza dough generously as you stretch. For this purpose, I use finely ground semolina and a small amount of rice flour. If you're having issues with sticky dough, try rice flour on your pizza peel. Rice flour works very well at preventing dough from sticking as it doesn't absorb water as easily as other flours and is mostly flavorless. Use caution and don't go overboard when dusting, excess flour dumped into the oven will burn, smoke, and cause undesirable flavors.

TO STRETCH A ROUND PIZZA BY HAND

Place a handful of semolina flour or a mix of semolina flour and rice flour on a work surface.

Lightly dust a flexible bench scraper and the top of the dough ball with the semolina or flour blend. Slide the scraper under the dough and cradle the dough with your hands as you transfer it to your floured work surface.

Flatten the dough gently, pushing flat with your hand on the center of the dough and leaving the outer edge of the dough untouched.

Leaving the direct center of the dough untouched at first, begin forming the crust. Push the air in, down, and out toward the edges gently. After the crust edge has begun to fill with air, push down in the center with your fingers.

Pick the dough up and drape it over your knuckles, top side up, preserving the outer crust. Rotate the dough, gently stretching as you go. Return the dough to the floured work surface and give it a few spins on the flour to make sure it isn't sticky.

Lightly dust a wooden pizza peel with rice flour. Transfer the stretched dough to the peel, giving it a final stretch in your hands as your transfer it. Once on the peel you have the chance to reshape a bit. Even out any uneven areas of the dough, pushing it out on peel, but be careful to not de-gas the puffy crust!

If the pizza shrinks significantly as you top it, the dough can be pulled out to the full size of the peel after topping. Carefully slip your fingers under the crust, carefully preserving the edge and stretching out toward the edges of the peel.

If the dough feels stuck to the peel after topping, carefully lift the edge of the crust up and sprinkle a small amount of rice flour under the dough. Shake, if it's still stuck, add more till you're able to easily shake it free.

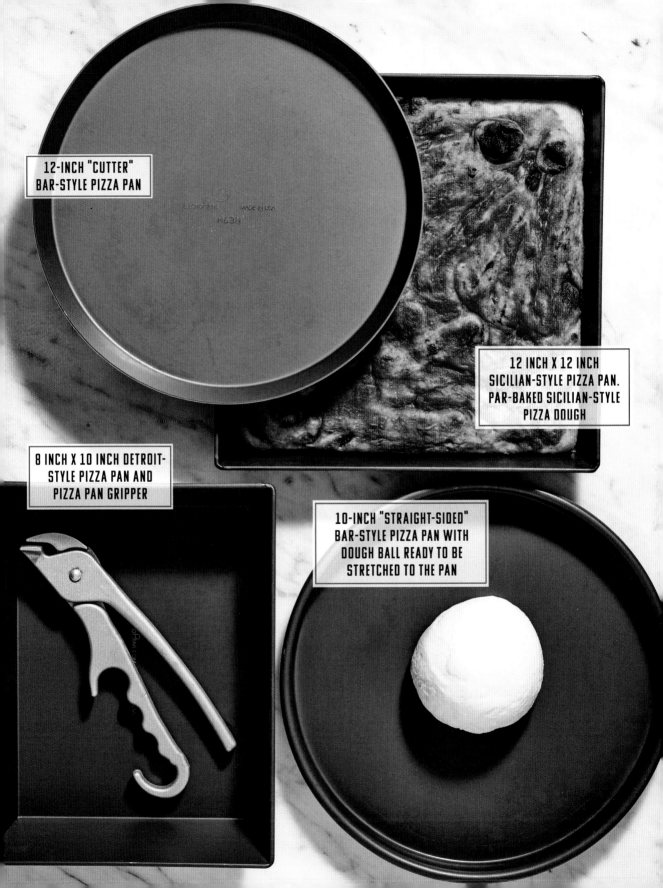

12-INCH "CUTTER" BAR-STYLE PIZZA PAN

12 INCH X 12 INCH SICILIAN-STYLE PIZZA PAN. PAR-BAKED SICILIAN-STYLE PIZZA DOUGH

8 INCH X 10 INCH DETROIT-STYLE PIZZA PAN AND PIZZA PAN GRIPPER

10-INCH "STRAIGHT-SIDED" BAR-STYLE PIZZA PAN WITH DOUGH BALL READY TO BE STRETCHED TO THE PAN

Chapter 1
New York–Style Pizzas

New York-style pizza is what many people think of as simply pizza. With a thin, crisp, yet still pliable crust, these pizzas are best enjoyed as a large slice, folded to eat.

New York–style pizza is hand tossed and baked directly on the oven stone. Using conduction to heat the baking surface, indoor pizza ovens excel at baking this style of pizza. They are closer to the deck-style ovens many New York–style pizzerias use—no tricks or hacks needed.

EQUIPMENT AND TOOLS

WOODEN PIZZA PEEL

For the New York–style pizzas, I build and top my pizzas on a wooden pizza peel. A wooden peel lightly dusted with semolina or rice flour should allow a fully topped pizza to slide right off and into the oven. Metal pizza peels become sticky quickly and should be reserved for quickly transferring pizzas, not stretching and building them.

PIZZA TURNING PEEL

A pizza turning peel is the best tool for turning and maneuvering New York–style pizza as it bakes. The turning peel keeps the pizza in the oven and in contact with the baking surface while turning. This result is a better baked pizza.

ROLLER PIZZA CUTTER

I slice my round pizzas with a classic, wheel-style pizza cutter. A high-quality cutter should produce clean-cut slices with little drag.

PIZZA SCREEN AND TRAY FOR SERVING

I serve my pizza on a pizza screen nested in a pizza tray to keep it crisp while serving. Slice the pizza on a cutting board before transferring.

NEW YORK-STYLE PIZZA
DOUGH

180 grams filtered water

9 grams kosher salt

1.5 grams instant dry yeast

6 grams extra-virgin olive oil

300 grams bread flour (Recommended: King Arthur Bread Flour or Central Milling "High Mountain" Flour)

1–2 teaspoons (5–10 ml) avocado oil or other neutral-flavored oil

C lassic New York–style pizza dough is perfect for a thin-crusted, foldable slice. It's a little crisp, but never dry. Like many doughs, this pizza dough benefits by an overnight or longer rest in the refrigerator. It's often best at around 48 hours of cold fermentation.

1 **At least 8 hours before baking pizza or preferably (cold fermented) 18 to 72 hours before:** Pour the filtered water into a large mixing bowl, add the salt, and stir to dissolve completely. Sprinkle the yeast on the surface of the water and let the yeast absorb some of the water for about 1 minute before stirring to dissolve completely. Pour in the olive oil and add the flour.

2 Using your hands, mix the ingredients, stirring and pinching with your fingers till all the ingredients are fully incorporated and no dry flour remains and the olive oil is well distributed. Do not knead at this point. Cover and let rest at room temperature (about 70°F [21°C]) for 20 to 30 minutes. This rest gives the flour some time to absorb the water and makes the dough easier to knead.

3 After 20 to 30 minutes, uncover the dough and knead for 2 to 3 minutes directly in the bowl or on a work surface till mostly smooth. Cover and let rest at room temperature (about 70°F [21°C]) for 1 to 2 hours.

4 After 1 to 2 hours, the dough should have risen some and look shiny. Uncover and knead the dough in the bowl or on a lightly floured work surface. Cover the dough while you prepare the dough tray, bowls, or plates. ➻

YIELD:
2 pizza dough balls for two 10-inch (25-cm) to 12-inch (30-cm) pizzas

5 Lightly coat your dough tray, plates, or bowls with a thin layer of neutral oil. It should be nicely slicked, but not pooled. Remove any excess oil with a paper towel. Uncover the dough and transfer to a work surface. Knead the dough a couple times and form into a large ball. Using a bench scraper, divide the dough into 2 equal portions (I use a scale for this). Form each portion into a dough ball by folding the edges of the dough into the center and repeating the process a few times until the tops of the dough balls are smooth. Pinch the dough balls closed with your fingers and place on your work surface.

6 Give each dough ball a couple spins with your hands to smooth out the bottom a bit. Transfer the dough balls to the oiled dough tray, bowls, or plates. Using a pastry brush, brush a thin coat of oil on the surface of each dough ball. Cover and transfer to the refrigerator to cold ferment for 18 to 72 hours. If using the dough the same day, cover but do not refrigerate and proceed with the next steps.

7 **2 to 4 hours before baking the pizzas:** Remove the dough tray, bowls, or plates from the refrigerator and let the dough rise, covered, at room temperature (about 70°F [21°C]) for 2 to 4 hours before stretching and baking. Look for the dough to have expanded and risen with lots of small bubbles on the surface.

NEW YORK-STYLE PIZZA
SAUCE

1 can (28 ounces, or 785 ml) whole peeled tomatoes

2 tablespoons (32 g) tomato paste

1 small clove garlic, minced

½ teaspoon dried oregano

¼ teaspoon garlic powder

Kosher salt to taste

The simple, comforting flavors of a slice joint sauce rarely fail to hit the spot. This multipurpose sauce is comfortable on a classic New York–style pizza and pretty much everywhere else pizza is found.

1 Combine the whole peeled tomatoes, tomato paste, garlic, oregano, and garlic powder in a 1-quart (946 ml) deli container. Blend with an immersion blender until mostly smooth.

2 Season to taste with kosher salt. The sauce can be stored in an airtight container in the refrigerator for up to a week.

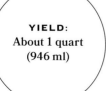

YIELD:
About 1 quart
(946 ml)

SPICY
VODKA SAUCE

2 tablespoons (28 g) unsalted butter

1 small yellow onion, diced

3 cloves garlic, diced

Kosher salt to taste

6–8 Calabrian chilis in oil, about ¼ cup (34 g), diced (add a few more for extra spicy)

⅓ cup (80 ml) vodka

1 tube (4.5 ounces, or 128 g) tomato paste

1 can (14 ounces, or 395 g) ground tomatoes (or whole peeled)

1 cup (235 ml) heavy cream

Freshly ground black pepper to taste

Calabrian chili peppers add a spicy, mildly smoky element to the sauce that makes it absolutely craveable. It's worth seeking them out at a specialty grocery store or ordering online. This spicy sauce is also amazing on pasta or topping crispy, cheese-covered chicken cutlets.

1 Melt the butter in 4-quart (3.8 L) saucepan or small stock pot over medium-low heat. Add the onions and garlic, season with a pinch of salt, and cook, stirring often till the onions and garlic are fully softened but not browned. Add the chopped Calabrian chilis and continue cooking for 3 to 5 minutes until mostly soft. Add the vodka and increase the heat to medium-high and cook for 2 to 3 minutes until slightly reduced.

2 Lower the heat to a simmer and stir in the tomato paste. Cook briefly till the paste is fully incorporated into the other ingredients. Add the ground tomatoes and bring to a simmer. Stirring occasionally, let cook till slightly reduced and thickened, about 10 minutes. Stir in the heavy cream and remove from heat.

3 Transfer to a blender and blend till completely smooth. Season to taste with kosher salt and black pepper. Add an additional Calabrian chili or two if the sauce needs some more heat. Let cool before topping pizza. The spicy vodka sauce can be stored in an airtight container in the refrigerator for up to 5 days.

YIELD:
About 1 quart
(946 ml)

EPIC
FOUR-CHEESE PIZZA

2 ounces (55 g) low-moisture whole-milk mozzarella cheese, thickly shredded

2 ounces (55 g) low-moisture part-skim mozzarella cheese, thickly shredded

1 New York–Style Pizza Dough ball (see p. 15)

3–4 ounces (90 to 120 ml) New York–Style Pizza Sauce (see p. 18)

¼ teaspoon dried oregano

⅓ cup (8 g) fresh basil leaves, plus more as needed

2 ounces (55 g) fresh mozzarella cheese

¼ cup (25 g) finely shredded Parmigiano Reggiano

Extra-virgin olive oil for drizzling the finished pizza

YIELD:
One 10-inch
(25-cm) to 12-inch
(30-cm) pizza

This is the cheese slice you will dream about. In this hybrid version of a "sauce topped" pizza, we add the shredded cheese before the sauce and top it with fresh mozzarella after to keep things nice and crisp.

1 Preheat your indoor pizza oven with the temperature set to 650°F (343°C). When fully heated, set the heat balance dial (if equipped) to Bottom 3/Top 7.

2 Mix the shredded cheeses in a bowl and set aside. Stretch your pizza dough to 10 to 12 inches (25 to 30 cm) (see stretching techniques p. 10). Scatter the cheese over the top of the pizza, leaving room for the crust. Use a spoon to dot the pizza with the sauce. Sprinkle the oregano and basil over the top. Distribute marble-sized chunks of mozzarella amongst the basil leaves.

3 The temperature of the baking stone should be around 650°F to 700°F (343°C to 371°C) when loading the pizza into the oven. Slide the pizza onto the center of the baking stone and bake for about 5 minutes, turning once or twice. You want the cheese to melt, but not become oily and burnt. If it begins to look too dark, adjust the heat balance dial one level at a time. When the cheese is melted and the crust and bottom of the pizza are golden brown with some darker spots, remove the pizza from the oven using a turning peel and transfer to a wire rack to let the crust set for about 1 minute.

4 Transfer the pizza to a wooden peel to slice and slide the pizza onto your serving tray or plate. Top with additional fresh basil leaves if you're feeling it, tearing them with your hands as you go. Add some Parmigiano Reggiano, drizzle with olive oil, and serve immediately.

SPICY VODKA
SLICE

1 New York–Style Pizza Dough ball (see p. 15)

4 ounces (120 ml) Spicy Vodka Sauce (see p. 19)

2 ounces (55 g) smoked mozzarella cheese, thickly shredded

4 ounces (115 g) fresh mozzarella cheese

1–3 Calabrian chili peppers, stems removed

⅓ cup (8 g) fresh basil leaves

¼ cup (25 g) finely shredded Parmigiano Reggiano

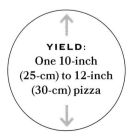

YIELD:
One 10-inch (25-cm) to 12-inch (30-cm) pizza

Rich, spicy, and a little smoky, this is a super satisfying slice. Spiked with vodka and Calabrian chiles, it's a party in every bite. The lightly creamy sauce mellows out the heat of the chiles a bit, a welcome relief for some. For me though, I want a little burn, so I typically toss a few extra chiles on the pie. Experiment and find your own level of fire.

1　Preheat your indoor pizza oven with the temperature set to 650°F (343°C). When fully heated, set the heat balance dial (if equipped) to Bottom 4/Top 6.

2　Stretch your pizza dough to 10 to 12 inches (25 to 30 cm) (see stretching techniques p. 10). Ladle or spoon the sauce into the center of the pizza and spread in a circular motion outward, leaving room for the crust to rise. Sprinkle the shredded cheese over the sauce, followed by the fresh mozzarella cheese, breaking off marble-size chunks with your hands. Place 1 chunk of fresh mozzarella in the center of the pizza and then place 4 to 5 additional pieces in a circle around the center, followed by 7 to 8 pieces just inside the crust. Place 1 whole Calabrian chili in the center of the pizza and scatter a few more around it if you like it spicy.

3　Check the temperature of the baking stone. It should be around 600°F to 650°F (316°C to 343°C) when loading the pizza into the oven. Very high heat can "break" creamy sauces like this spicy vodka sauce, so make sure the oven is not overheated by checking with an infrared thermometer before loading the pizza. Slide the pizza onto the center of the baking stone and bake for about 5 minutes, turning once. You want the cheese to melt but not darken. If the bottom or top begins to look too dark, adjust the heat balance dial one level at a time. ➡

4 When the cheese is melted and the crust and bottom of the pizza are golden brown with some darker spots, remove the pizza from the oven using a turning peel and transfer to a wire rack to let the crust set for about 1 minute.

5 Transfer the pizza to a wooden peel to slice and slide the pizza onto your serving tray or plate. Top with the fresh basil leaves, tearing them with your hands as you go. Shower the pizza with the shredded Parmigiano Reggiano and serve immediately.

BROCCOLI RANCH
PIZZA

1 small head of broccoli, broken into small florets

2 tablespoons (28 ml) extra-virgin olive oil

3 tablespoons (30 g) ranch seasoning, divided

Freshly ground black pepper to taste

Kosher salt to taste

2 ounces (55 g) low-moisture part-skim mozzarella cheese, thickly shredded

2 ounces (55 g) Havarti cheese with dill, thickly shredded

1 New York–Style Pizza Dough ball (see p. 15)

2 ounces (71 ml) New York–Style Pizza Sauce (see p. 18)

¼ cup (60 ml) ranch dressing

YIELD:
One 10-inch (25-cm) to 12-inch (30-cm) pizza

Take a trip to the Broccoli Ranch. Near pizza, ranch dressing in any form can cause some strife. Here, we double-down with ranch-roasted broccoli and a post-bake ranch dressing drizzle for a trip deep down into Hidden Valley.

1 **To make the Ranch-Roasted Broccoli:** Preheat a home oven to 375°F (190°C, or gas mark 5). Toss the broccoli florets with the olive oil and 2 tablespoons (20 g) of the ranch seasoning and black pepper. Scatter the florets on a sheet pan and roast till just tender, 7 to 10 minutes. Remove the roasted broccoli from the pan and season to taste with kosher salt. Let cool before topping the pizza. Ranch-Roasted Broccoli can be stored in an airtight container in the refrigerator for 3 to 5 days.

2 **To make the pizza:** Preheat your indoor pizza oven with the temperature set to 650°F (343°C). When fully heated, set the heat balance dial (if equipped) to Bottom 3/Top 7.

3 Mix the shredded cheeses in a bowl and set aside. Stretch your pizza dough to 10 to 12 inches (25 to 30 cm) (see stretching techniques p. 10). Ladle or spoon the sauce into the center of the pizza and spread in a circular motion outward, leaving room for the crust to rise. Scatter the shredded cheese mixture over the sauce, followed by the roasted broccoli florets.

4 Check the temperature of the baking stone. It should be around 650°F to 700°F (343°C to 371°C) when loading the pizza into the oven. Slide the pizza onto the center of the baking stone and bake for about 5 minutes, turning once or twice. You want the ➤➤

cheese to melt fully but not "break" or darken too much. If the bottom or top begins to look too dark, adjust the heat balance dial one level at a time.

5 When the broccoli is charred in some spots and the cheese is melted on a golden-brown crust with a few dark spots on the top and bottom, remove the pizza from the oven using a turning peel and transfer to a wire rack to let the crust set for about 1 minute.

6 Transfer the pizza to a wooden peel to slice and slide the pizza onto your serving tray or plate. Sprinkle the rest of the ranch seasoning over the pizza and drizzle with ranch dressing. Serve immediately with additional ranch dressing for dipping, if that's your thing.

THE ITALIAN HERO

½ cup (125 g) cherry tomatoes, halved crosswise

1 clove garlic, minced

¼ cup (60 ml) extra-virgin olive oil, additional for drizzling

½ teaspoon dried oregano, divided

Kosher salt to taste

Freshly ground black pepper to taste

1 New York–Style Pizza Dough ball (see p. 15)

4 slices provolone cheese

2 slices rosemary ham, cut into thin strips

6 slices smoked salami (or a mild salami such as Genoa)

8 slices Calabrese salami

15 slices cupping pepperoni

¼ cup (29 g) thinly sliced red onion

1 roasted red bell pepper, cut into thin strips

¼ cup (30 g) sliced pepperoncini, drained

¼ cup (60 g) cherry peppers, drained

½ cup (12 g) fresh basil leaves

1 ball fresh burrata cheese (about 4 ounces, or 115 g)

4 slices prosciutto di Parma

Red wine vinegar or balsamic vinegar (optional)

This Italian Hero is a pizza topped with all the flavors of a classic Italian hero sandwich. Fold up a slice and experience an iconic New York sandwich and pizza at the same time. This pizza is completely stacked with the quintessential flavors of the sub. The stacked layers of toppings mean the pizza may take a little more baking time than usual. Make sure to give the pizza longer than a New York minute to melt the cheese and let the flavors fully combine.

1 Place the halved cherry tomatoes and minced garlic in a small bowl. Drizzle the tomatoes and garlic with ¼ cup (60 ml) of extra-virgin olive oil and season with ¼ teaspoon of oregano. Toss well to combine. Season to taste with kosher salt and black pepper. Set aside till ready to top the pizza.

2 Preheat your indoor pizza oven with the temperature set to 650°F (343°C). When fully heated, set the heat balance dial (if equipped) to Bottom 3/Top 7.

3 Stretch your pizza dough to 10 to 12 inches (25 to 30 cm) (see stretching techniques p. 10). Leaving room for the crust to rise, arrange the 4 slices of provolone cheese to cover as much of the pizza as possible, overlapping in some spots. Scatter the sliced rosemary ham over the cheese. Place one slice of smoked salami in the center of the pizza and the 5 additional slices around it. Arrange 3 slices of the Calabrese salami in a ring around the center of the pizza and an additional 5 slices in a ring closer to the crust. Scatter the 15 slices of pepperoni over the top, filling in any gaps left by the other salami.

4 Top the pizza with the tomato mixture, red onions, roasted red pepper, pepperoncini, and cherry peppers. Drizzle with extra-virgin olive oil and ¼ teaspoon of oregano. ➻

YIELD:
One 10-inch
(25-cm) to 12-inch
(30-cm) pizza

5 Check the temperature of the baking stone. It should be around 650°F to 700°F (343°C to 371°C) when loading the pizza into the oven. Slide the pizza onto the center of the baking stone and bake for 5 to 6 minutes, turning once or twice. This pizza is loaded with toppings, so it might take it a little longer than other pizzas of this style. Make sure the cheese is fully melted before removing from the oven and transferring to a wire rack to let the crust set for about 1 minute.

6 Transfer the pizza to a wooden peel to slice and slide the pizza onto your serving tray or plate. Tear the basil leaves directly onto the finished pizza adding a generous amount on each slice. Using your hands, break off large chunks of burrata, placing one on each slice. Drape the prosciutto di Parma over the burrata, about ½ slice of prosciutto on each slice. Drizzle with extra-virgin olive oil and vinegar (optional) and season with a pinch of oregano and few cranks of black pepper. Serve immediately.

BUFFALO CHICKEN
PIZZA

FOR THE BUFFALO CHICKEN:
2 ounces (55 g) unsalted butter, melted

½ cup (60 ml) Frank's Red Hot Original Cayenne Pepper Sauce (not the "Buffalo Wings Sauce")

8 ounces (225 g) cooked shredded chicken

FOR THE PIZZA:
2 ounces (55 g) low-moisture whole-milk mozzarella cheese, thickly shredded

2 ounces (55 g) Monterey Jack cheese, thickly shredded

1 New York–Style Pizza Dough ball (see p. 15)

2 ounces (55 g) Maytag blue cheese, crumbled

¼ cup (25 g) green onions, thinly sliced, divided

1 tablespoon (4 g) celery leaves

¼ cup (60 ml) blue cheese dressing or ranch dressing

Freshly ground black pepper to taste

YIELD:
One 10-inch (25-cm) to 12-inch (30-cm) pizza

The tangy, spicy vibe of Buffalo-style wing sauce is addictive on pizza. I keep close to the traditional preparation with a simple wing sauce made of hot sauce mounted with butter.

1 **To make the Buffalo Chicken:** Melt the butter in a small saucepan over low heat. Once melted, remove from the heat and whisk in the hot sauce. Combine the cooked chicken and Buffalo sauce in a bowl. Set aside. The chicken can be stored in an airtight container in the refrigerator for 3 to 4 days.

2 **To make the pizza:** Preheat your indoor pizza oven with the temperature set to 650°F (343°C). When fully heated, set the heat balance dial (if equipped) to Bottom 3/Top 7.

3 Combine the shredded cheeses. Stretch your pizza dough to 10 to 12 inches (25 to 30 cm) (see stretching techniques p. 10). Top the pizza with the cheese mixture, leaving room for the crust, followed by the crumbled blue cheese. Top with the Buffalo Chicken and half of the green onions.

4 Check the temperature of the baking stone. It should be around 650°F to 700°F (343°C to 371°C). Slide the pizza onto the center of the baking stone and bake for about 5 minutes, turning once or twice. Adjust the balance dial if the top is getting too dark.

5 When the cheese is melted and the crust is baked, remove the pizza from the oven and transfer to a wire rack to let the crust set for about 1 minute. Slice the pizza and slide it onto your serving tray or plate. Top with the celery leaves and drizzle with blue cheese or ranch dressing and a few cracks of fresh black pepper. Serve immediately with more blue cheese or ranch dressing on the side for dunking.

SESAME SEED-CRUST SAUCE TOP PIZZA
WITH SAUSAGE

1 New York–Style Pizza Dough ball (see p. 15)

2 tablespoons (28 ml) avocado oil or other neutral oil

3 tablespoons (24 g) sesame seeds

4 ounces (115 g) fresh mozzarella cheese

Small handful fresh basil leaves, divided

6 ounces (170 g) homemade Fennel Sausage (see p. 67) or sweet Italian sausage

4 ounces (120 ml) New York–Style Pizza Sauce (see p. 18)

¼ cup (25 g) finely shredded Parmigiano Reggiano

Extra-virgin olive oil, for drizzling the finished pizza

Sesame seeds on the crust add texture and flavor to this "sauce topped" sausage pizza. Topping the pizza "upside down" helps keep the crust nice and crisp. It's perfect for loading it up with a generous amount of homemade Fennel Sausage (see p. 67). It's a simple slice, but one that's loaded with flavor. If you struggle with soggy bottom pizza, going "sauce on top" may just be your solution.

1 Preheat your indoor pizza oven with the temperature set to 650°F (343°C). When fully heated, set the heat balance dial (if equipped) to Bottom 3/Top 7.

2 Stretch your pizza dough to 10 to 12 inches (25 to 30 cm) (see stretching techniques p. 10). Using a pastry brush, brush the outer rim of the crust (about an inch [2.5 cm] from the edge) with the avocado oil. Take care to not drip too much excess oil onto your pizza peel. Using the palm of your hand to prevent the sesame seeds from scattering everywhere, cradle the outside of the crust while you apply them to the oiled portion of the dough.

3 Top the pizza with the fresh mozzarella cheese, breaking it into marble-size chunks with your hands as you go. Scatter the basil leaves over the cheese, tearing any especially large leaves. Top the pizza with the fresh sausage in small marble-size chunks. Using a ladle or a spoon, dot the top of the pizza with the sauce all over.

4 Check the temperature of the baking stone. It should be around 650°F to 700°F (343°C to 371°C) when loading the pizza into the oven. Slide the pizza onto the center of the baking stone and bake for about 5 minutes, turning once or twice. Look for the cheese to melt and the sausage to brown and crisp slightly.

YIELD:
One 10-inch (25-cm) to 12-inch (30-cm) pizza

5 When the top and bottom of the pizza crust are golden brown with a few darker spots and the sausage is cooked through, remove the pizza from the oven using a turning peel and transfer to a wire rack to let the crust set for about 1 minute.

6 Transfer the pizza to a wooden peel to slice and slide the pizza onto your serving tray or plate. Top with additional basil leaves, a shower of Parmigiano Reggiano, and a drizzle of extra-virgin olive oil. Serve immediately.

Chapter 2
Artisan Pizzas

These pizzas journey beyond the world of red sauce to a universe where pizza dough is the ultimate culinary canvas. These recipes may push the boundaries of what you typically expect to see on pizza, but trust me, they're delicious. Creative and "outside the box" pizza recipes are the ones that I find the most fun to develop. I have an insatiable curiosity, and I love to scour the world and my local farmer's market for the next greatest pizza toppings. I hope you have fun exploring these pizza adventures.

EQUIPMENT AND TOOLS

WOODEN PIZZA PEEL

For the artisan-style pizzas, I like to build and top my pizzas on a wooden pizza peel. A wooden peel lightly dusted with rice flour should allow a fully topped pizza to slide right off and into the oven. Metal pizza peels can stick easily and should be reserved for quickly transferring pizzas, not stretching and building them.

PIZZA TURNING PEEL

A pizza turning peel is the best tool for turning and maneuvering artisan pizza as it bakes. The turning peel keeps the pizza in the oven and in contact with the baking surface while turning. This results in a better baked pizza.

ROLLER PIZZA CUTTER

I slice my round pizzas with a classic, wheel-style pizza cutter. A high-quality cutter should produce clean-cut slices with little drag.

PIZZA SCREEN AND TRAY FOR SERVING

I serve my pizza on a pizza screen nested in a pizza tray to keep it crisp while serving. Slice the pizza on a cutting board before transferring.

ARTISAN PIZZA
DOUGH

225 grams filtered water

11 grams kosher salt

2 grams instant dry yeast

10 grams extra-virgin olive oil, plus more as needed

5 grams honey

350 grams bread flour (Recommended: King Arthur Bread Flour or Central Milling "High Mountain" Flour)

5 grams dark rye flour

T his is my go-to "daily dough." Delicious, easy to prepare, and super versatile, this dough is perfect for the fully loaded pizza recipes in this chapter or can be used in the New York–style or Neapolitan-style recipes. A small amount of rye flour deepens the flavor of this dough and helps speed along the fermentation process.

1 **At least 8 hours before baking pizza or preferably (cold fermented) 18 to 72 hours before:** Pour the filtered water into a large mixing bowl, add the salt, and stir to dissolve completely. Sprinkle the yeast on the surface of the water and let the yeast absorb some of the water for about 1 minute before stirring to dissolve completely. Add the honey to the bowl and stir to dissolve. Pour in the olive oil and add both the flours.

2 Using your hands, mix the ingredients, stirring and pinching with your fingers till all the ingredients are fully incorporated and no dry flour remains and the olive oil is well distributed. Do not knead at this point. Cover and let rest at room temperature (about 70°F [21°C]) for 20 to 30 minutes. This rest gives the flour some time to absorb the water and makes the dough easier to knead.

3 After 20 to 30 minutes, uncover the dough and knead for 2 to 3 minutes directly in the bowl or on a work surface till mostly smooth. Cover and let rest at room temperature (about 70°F [21°C]) for 1 to 2 hours.

4 After 1 hour, the dough should have risen some and look mostly shiny. Uncover the dough and pick up the dough ball. It should feel lighter now, like it has some air in it. Knead the dough in the bowl using your hands, de-gassing any large bubbles that may have formed. Cover and let rest for about 30 minutes. ➻

YIELD:
2 pizza dough balls for two 10-inch (25-cm) to 12-inch (30-cm) pizzas

5 Uncover and lightly knead the dough in the bowl using your hands. Cover the dough while you prepare the dough tray, bowls, or plates.

6 Lightly coat your dough tray, plates, or bowls with a thin layer of oil. It should be nicely slicked, but not pooled. Remove any excess oil with a paper towel.

7 Uncover the dough and transfer to a work surface. Knead the dough a couple times and form into a large ball. Using a bench scraper, divide the dough into 2 equal portions (I use a scale for this). Form each portion into a dough ball by folding the edges of the dough into the center and repeating the process a few times until the tops of the dough balls are smooth. Pinch the dough balls closed with your fingers and place on your work surface. Give each dough ball a couple spins with your hands to smooth out the bottom a bit.

8 Transfer the dough balls to the oiled dough tray, bowls, or plates. Using a pastry brush, brush a thin coat of oil on the surface of each dough ball. Cover and transfer to the refrigerator to cold ferment for 18 to 72 hours. If using the dough the same day, cover but do not refrigerate and proceed with the next steps.

9 **4 to 6 hours before baking the pizzas:** Remove the dough tray, bowls, or plates from the refrigerator and let the dough rise, covered, at room temperature (about 70°F [21°C]) for 4 to 6 hours before stretching and baking. Look for the dough to have expanded and risen with lots of small bubbles on the surface.

SMASHED POTATO AND CHORIZO PIZZA
WITH CILANTRO-LIME CREMA

FOR THE SMASHED POTATOES:

1 teaspoon apple cider vinegar

Kosher salt

1 pound (455 g) fingerling potatoes

1 to 2 tablespoons (15 to 28 ml) extra-virgin olive oil

Freshly ground black pepper to taste

FOR THE CILANTRO-LIME CREMA:

2 tablespoons (30 g) sour cream

1 tablespoon (1 g) finely chopped cilantro

1 lime, zested and juiced

FOR THE PIZZA:

1 Artisan Pizza Dough ball (see p. 35)

18 slices dry chorizo (Spanish style)

2 ounces (55 g) Mahón or Manchego cheese, thickly shredded

3 ounces (85 g) fresh mozzarella cheese pearls

1 small shallot, thinly sliced

2 roasted piquillo peppers, diced

2 green onions, thinly sliced, white and green parts separated

1 tablespoon (1 g) finely chopped cilantro

Choripapa is a simple and satisfying dish of chorizo and crispy potatoes found throughout Latin America. The preparation varies by location. Sliced, cured chorizo is common in some locales while others opt for the fresh, crumbly variety. The potatoes vary as well, from frozen French fries to home fries. When something is this delicious in any form, I have to put it on a pizza. For my version, I use cured, sliced chorizo and crispy, smashed potatoes, and the result is this drool-inducing pizza. Looking for a variation? Toss an egg on it and call it breakfast.

1 **To make the Smashed Potatoes:** Fill a pot with water, add the vinegar and a generous pinch of kosher salt, and bring to a boil. Add the potatoes and cook till tender, about 20 minutes. Heat your home oven to 400°F (200°C, or gas mark 6). Drain the potatoes in a colander and allow to dry and cool down for a few minutes. Transfer the potatoes to a sheet pan and smash with the bottom of another sheet. Transfer the potatoes to a bowl. Drizzle with olive oil and season to taste with kosher salt and black pepper. Transfer to a sheet pan and roast in the oven till golden brown and crispy. Let cool to room temperature before topping pizza. The smashed potatoes can be stored in an airtight container in the refrigerator for 3 to 4 days.

2 **To make the Cilantro-Lime Crema:** Add the sour cream, cilantro, and lime juice and zest to a small bowl. Whisk well to combine. Set aside till ready to top the finished pizza. The crema can be stored in an airtight container in the refrigerator for 2 weeks or more. ➤➤

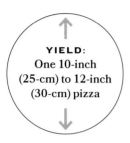

YIELD:
One 10-inch
(25-cm) to 12-inch
(30-cm) pizza

3 **To make the pizza:** Preheat your indoor pizza oven with the temperature set to 700°F (370°C). When fully heated, set the heat balance dial (if equipped) to Bottom 3/Top 7.

4 Stretch your pizza dough to 10 to 12 inches (25 to 30 cm) (see stretching techniques p. 10). Place 1 slice of chorizo in the center of the pizza, 6 slices around it, and the remaining 11 slices in a circle just inside the crust. Sprinkle the shredded cheese over the chorizo-topped pizza, followed by the fresh mozzarella cheese pearls. Top with the Smashed Potatoes, breaking them up into smaller, craggy chunks with your hands. Scatter the shallots all over the pizza along with the diced peppers and white parts of the green onions.

5 Check the temperature of the baking stone. It should be around 700°F to 750°F (370°C to 399°C) when loading the pizza into the oven. Slide the pizza onto the center of the baking stone and bake for about 5 minutes, turning a few times with a turning peel for an even bake.

6 When fully baked, the bottom of the crust should be browned and dark in some spots. The top of the crust should be a pleasing golden brown with lots of micro-blisters that may have darkened in a few spots, and the cheese should be fully melted. Remove the pizza from the oven using a turning peel and transfer to a wire rack to let the crust set for about 1 minute.

7 Transfer the pizza to a wooden peel to slice and slide the pizza onto your serving tray or plate. Sprinkle the cilantro and green onions all over the sliced pizza. Drizzle with the Cilantro-Lime Crema and serve immediately.

HAM AND BRIE WITH CARAMELIZED ONIONS
AND MUSTARD CREAM PIZZA

FOR THE CARAMELIZED ONIONS:

2 tablespoons (28 ml) avocado or other neutral-flavored oil

2 large yellow onions, sliced ¼" thick (0.6 cm)

¼ teaspoon kosher salt, plus more as needed

2 tablespoons to ¼ cup (28 ml to 60 ml) water, to deglaze the pan

Freshly ground black pepper to taste

FOR THE MUSTARD CREAM:

½ cup (112 g) crème fraiche

2 tablespoons (28 ml) heavy cream

1 tablespoon (15 g) Dijon mustard

1 tablespoon (15 g) whole-grain mustard

2–3 chives, minced

Kosher salt to taste

Freshly ground black pepper to taste

The first-rate, rich and creamy pairing of ham and brie is made perfect on pizza crust. The ham is sliced into strips, giving it more edge area to crisp as it bakes and slides into the tangy mustard cream below. A little bit elegant, this pizza doesn't feel out of place at a holiday party or served as part of a dinner with a crisp green salad.

1 **To make the Caramelized Onions:** Heat the oil in a heavy-bottom pot over medium-high heat. Add the onions, stir to coat in the oil, and sprinkle with ¼ teaspoon kosher salt. After the onions have softened and released some of their liquid, reduce the heat to low and continue cooking, stirring often until the onions are golden brown and caramelized, about 45 minutes. Use the water to deglaze the pan as you caramelize the onions to prevent them from sticking to the pan and burning. Transfer the onions to a bowl to cool and season to taste with kosher salt and black pepper. The Caramelized Onions can be stored in an airtight container in the refrigerator for up to 4 days.

2 **To make the Mustard Cream:** Combine the crème fraiche, heavy cream, Dijon mustard, and whole-grain mustard in a bowl and whisk to combine. Fold in the chives and season to taste with kosher salt and black pepper. Set aside until ready to top the pizza. The Mustard Cream can be stored in an airtight container in the refrigerator for at least a week.

3 **To make the pizza:** Preheat your indoor pizza oven with the temperature set to 700°F (370°C). When fully heated, set the heat balance dial (if equipped) to Bottom 3/Top 7.

FOR THE PIZZA:
1 Artisan Pizza Dough ball (see p. 35)

4 ounces (115 g) Brie cheese, cut into small chunks

4 ounces (115 g) sliced French ham, cut into strips

2–3 chives, minced

½ teaspoon minced parsley

4 Stretch your pizza dough to 10 to 12 inches (25 to 30 cm) (see stretching techniques p. 10). Spread the Mustard Cream all over the pizza, leaving room for the crust to rise. Top the Mustard Cream with the Brie cheese, followed by the Caramelized Onions. Scatter the strips of ham all over the pizza.

5 Check the temperature of the baking stone. It should be around 700°F to 750°F (370°C to 399°C) when loading the pizza into the oven. Slide the pizza onto the center of the baking stone and bake for 4 to 5 minutes, turning the pizza a few times with a turning peel for an even bake.

6 Look for the bottom of the crust to be browned and dark in some spots. The top of the crust should be golden brown with melted cheese and a few crispy bits of ham should be visible.

7 When fully baked, remove the pizza from the oven using a turning peel and transfer to a wire rack to let the crust set for about 1 minute.

8 Transfer the pizza to a wooden peel to slice into 6 or 8 slices and slide the pizza onto your serving tray or plate. Sprinkle the pizza with the chives and parsley. Serve immediately.

YIELD:
One 10-inch (25-cm) to 12-inch (30-cm) pizza

THE MUFFULETTA
PIZZA

FOR THE OLIVE SALAD:

½ cup (85 g) pitted mixed olives

¼ cup (60 g) Italian-style giardiniera

¼ cup (30 g) sliced pepperoncini peppers

2 tablespoons (23 g) chopped roasted red peppers

1 small clove garlic, minced

1 teaspoon lemon juice and zest from 1 small lemon

2 teaspoons sherry vinegar

1 tablespoon (4 g) fresh parsley

¼ teaspoon dried oregano

2 tablespoons (28 ml) extra-virgin olive oil

Kosher salt to taste

Freshly ground black pepper to taste

FOR THE PIZZA:

1 Artisan Pizza Dough ball (see p. 35)

2 tablespoons (28 ml) avocado oil or other neutral oil

3 tablespoons (24 g) sesame seeds

2 ounces (55 g) fresh mozzarella cheese

2 ounces (55 g) provolone cheese, shredded

¼ pound (115 g) sliced genoa salami

The iconic New Orleans sandwich gets the pizza treatment. The sesame seed–studded sandwich traces its origins to early twentieth century Sicilian immigrants. In an alternate universe, it may have ended up a pizza. Here, we keep close to the original sandwich ingredients, including the signature sesame seed crust.

1 **To make the Olive Salad (best made 24 hours before making pizza):** Combine the olives, Italian-style giardiniera, pepperoncini, roasted red peppers, and garlic in the bowl of a small food processor. Pulse until fully chopped. Transfer the mix to a bowl, add the lemon juice and zest, vinegar, parsley, oregano, and olive oil. Mix well to combine. Season to taste with kosher salt and black pepper. Cover and transfer to the refrigerator. The Olive Salad is best after a 24-hour rest, but it can be used the same day. Allow it to rest at least an hour for the flavors to combine. The Olive Salad can be stored in an airtight container in the refrigerator for a month or more.

2 **To make the pizza:** Preheat your indoor pizza oven with the temperature set to 700°F (370°C). When fully heated, set the heat balance dial (if equipped) to Bottom 3/Top 7.

3 Stretch your pizza dough to 10 to 12 inches (25 to 30 cm) (see stretching techniques p. 10). Using a pastry brush, brush the outer rim of the crust (about an inch [2.5 cm] from the edge) with the avocado oil. Take care to not drip too much excess oil onto your pizza peel. Using the palm of your hand to prevent the sesame seeds from scattering everywhere, cradle the outside of the crust while you apply them to the oiled portion of the dough.

¼ pound (115 g) sliced capicola

¼ pound (115 g) sliced ham, cut into strips

¼ pound (115 g) sliced mortadella, cut into strips

Small handful fresh basil

Extra-virgin olive oil for drizzling the finished pizza

Freshly ground black pepper to taste

4 Top the pizza with ¼ cup to ½ cup of the Olive Salad, leaving room for the crust to rise. You want to make sure it ends up in every bite. Top the pizza with the fresh mozzarella cheese, breaking it into marble-size chunks with your hands as you go, followed by the shredded provolone cheese. Add the sliced salami and capicola to the top of the pizza, followed by the strips of ham and mortadella. You won't use it all. Save the additional for topping another pizza, sandwich, or panini.

5 Check the temperature of the baking stone. It should be around 700°F to 750°F (370°C to 399°C) when loading the pizza into the oven. Slide the pizza onto the center of the baking stone and bake for about 5 minutes, turning a few times with a turning peel for an even bake.

6 Look for the bottom of the crust to be browned and dark in some spots. The top of the crust should be golden brown, the cheese should be melted, and the salami should be crispy.

7 When fully baked, remove the pizza from the oven using a turning peel and transfer to a wire rack to let the crust set for about 1 minute.

8 Transfer the pizza to a wooden peel to slice into 6 or 8 slices and slide the pizza onto your serving tray or plate. Tear the basil leaves directly onto the finished pizza. Top each slice with a small spoonful of the Olive Salad, a drizzle of extra-virgin olive oil, and a few cracks of freshly ground black pepper. Serve immediately.

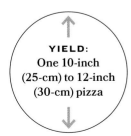

YIELD:
One 10-inch
(25-cm) to 12-inch
(30-cm) pizza

SPICY CHICKEN AND THAI BASIL
PIZZA

FOR THE SPICY CHICKEN AND THAI BASIL TOPPING:

¼ cup (60 ml) water or chicken stock

1 tablespoon (15 ml) soy sauce

1 tablespoon (15 ml) oyster sauce

2 teaspoons fish sauce

2 teaspoons palm sugar (or use brown sugar if unavailable)

1 tablespoon (15 ml) avocado or other neutral flavored oil

1 pound (455 g) ground chicken

3–4 Thai chiles (or use serrano if unavailable)

1 shallot, thinly sliced

3 cloves garlic, minced

1 bunch Thai (or holy) basil, leaves only (about 1½ cups [36 g]), divided

FOR THE PIZZA:

1 Artisan Pizza Dough ball (see p. 35)

¼ cup (60 ml) serrano chili oil a.k.a. Hot Oil (see p. 134), for brushing the crust

4 ounces (115 g) fresh mozzarella cheese

¼ cup Pickled Shallots, drained (see p. 88)

6–8 Holy (Thai) basil leaves, reserved from above

*P*ad krapow gai lands near the top on my list of Thai food cravings. The combination of minced chicken and fresh Thai basil slicked with a spicy, sweet, and salty sauce always has me reaching for more. It's a comforting dish that feels right at home served up on a pizza.

1   **To make the Spicy Chicken and Thai Basil Topping:** Using a whisk, mix the water or stock, soy sauce, oyster sauce, fish sauce, and sugar in a small bowl until fully blended. Set aside.

2   Heat the oil in a large skillet or wok over high heat. Add the chicken and cook until no longer pink, stirring often, about 3 minutes. Add the chiles, shallot, and garlic and cook, stirring often, till softened, about 3 minutes. Add the sauce to the pan and deglaze, scraping up any bits stuck to the pan, and cook, stirring often, till the sauce has thickened and glazed the ingredients, about 3 minutes. Turn the heat off, stir in all but 6 to 8 leaves of the Thai basil, and transfer to a bowl to cool before topping the pizza or store in an airtight container in the refrigerator for 3 to 4 days.

3   **To make the pizza:** Preheat your indoor pizza oven with the temperature set to 700°F (370°C). When fully heated, set the heat balance dial (if equipped) to Bottom 3/Top 7.

4   Stretch your pizza dough to 10 to 12 inches (25 to 30 cm) (see stretching techniques p. 10).Using a pastry brush, brush the outer rim of the crust (about an inch [2.5 cm] from the edge) with the serrano chili oil. Scatter the fresh mozzarella over the top of the pizza, breaking it into marble-size pieces with your hands as you go. Top with the Spicy Chicken and Thai Basil Topping. ➤➤

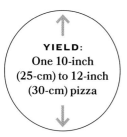

YIELD:
One 10-inch
(25-cm) to 12-inch
(30-cm) pizza

5 Check the temperature of the baking stone. It should be around 700°F to 750°F (370°C to 399°C) when loading the pizza into the oven. Slide the pizza onto the center of the baking stone and bake for about 5 minutes, turning a few times with a turning peel for an even bake.

6 When fully baked, the bottom of crust should be browned and dark in some spots. The top of the crust should be a pleasing golden brown with lots of micro-blisters that may have darkened in a few spots, and the cheese should be fully melted. Remove the pizza from the oven using a turning peel and transfer to a wire rack to let the crust set for about 1 minute.

7 Transfer the pizza to a wooden peel to slice and slide the pizza onto your serving tray or plate. Top the pizza with the Pickled Shallots and remaining basil leaves. Serve immediately.

THE SHAWARMA
SLICE

FOR THE SHAWARMA TOPPING:

8 ounces (225 g) gyro slices, chopped

1 small red onion, sliced

1 red bell pepper, sliced

1 tablespoon minced fresh parsley

FOR THE SPICY HARISSA SAUCE:

½ cup (60 g) tzatziki sauce

1–2 tablespoons (16 to 32 g) harissa pepper paste

FOR THE PIZZA:

½ cup (125 g) cherry tomatoes, halved

1 clove garlic, minced

¼ teaspoon dried oregano

1 tablespoon (28 ml) extra-virgin olive oil

1 teaspoon red wine vinegar

Kosher salt to taste

Freshly ground black pepper to taste

1 Artisan Pizza Dough ball (see p. 35)

3 ounces (85 g) fresh mozzarella cheese

¼ cup (38 g) crumbled feta cheese

2 tablespoons Pickled Shallots, drained (see p. 88)

Minced fresh parsley

Shawarma, the fragrant, crisp meat cooked on a vertical spit and wrapped in thin bread with an assortment of fresh, pickled, and spicy stuff, can be difficult to replicate at home. Making pizza the vessel for this favorite foldable feast makes bringing the flavors home easy. True shawarma-style meat can be difficult to find. Here, I'm using gyro slices, which can be found at Trader Joe's and other grocery stores. Crisped up with onions and peppers, it makes for a delicious pizza topping.

1 **To make the Shawarma Topping:** Heat a large skillet over medium-high heat. Add the chopped gyro meat. Let cook for 1 to 2 minutes undisturbed to let it render some of the fat, stir, and then continuing cooking, stirring often until browned. Transfer to a bowl using a slotted spoon, reserving about 1 tablespoon (15 ml) of the rendered fat. Reduce the heat to medium and add the onion and bell pepper and cook, stirring often till very soft. Transfer to the bowl of gyro meat and add the parsley. Stir to combine and set aside until ready to top the pizza. The Shawarma Topping can be stored in an airtight container in the refrigerator for up to 3 days.

2 **To make the Spicy Harissa Sauce:** Combine the tzatziki sauce and harissa and mix well. Set aside until ready to top the pizza. The Spicy Harissa Sauce can be stored in an airtight container in the refrigerator for 3 to 4 days.

3 **To make the pizza:** Combine the cherry tomatoes, garlic, oregano, olive oil, and vinegar in a bowl. Mix well to combine and season to taste with kosher salt and black pepper. Set aside until ready to top the pizza. ➛

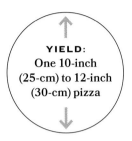

YIELD:
One 10-inch
(25-cm) to 12-inch
(30-cm) pizza

4 Preheat your indoor pizza oven with the temperature set to 700°F (370°C). When fully heated, set the heat balance dial (if equipped) to Bottom 3/Top 7.

5 Stretch your pizza dough to 10 to 12 inches (25 to 30 cm) (see stretching techniques p. 10). Leaving room for the crust to rise, top the pizza with the fresh mozzarella cheese, breaking it into marble-size chunks with your hands as you go, followed by the feta cheese. Scatter the Shawarma Topping all over the pizza.

6 Check the temperature of the baking stone. It should be around 700°F to 750°F (370°C to 399°C) when loading the pizza into the oven. Slide the pizza onto the center of the baking stone and bake for about 5 minutes, turning a few times with a turning peel for an even bake.

7 When fully baked, the bottom of crust should be browned and dark in some spots. The top of the crust should be golden brown with some dark spots, the cheese should be melted, and the meat should be crispy in some spots.

8 When fully baked, remove the pizza from the oven using a turning peel and transfer to a wire rack to let the crust set for about 1 minute.

9 Transfer the pizza to a wooden peel to slice into 6 or 8 slices and slide the pizza onto your serving tray or plate. Top each slice with some of the Pickled Shallots and a dollop of the Spicy Harissa Sauce. Sprinkle the parsley over the top of the pizza and serve immediately.

SMOKED SALMON PIZZA WITH CRISPY CAPERS AND HORSERADISH-AND-CHIVE CREAM
ON EVERYTHING BAGEL CRUST

FOR THE HORSERADISH-AND-CHIVE CREAM:

½ cup (60 ml) heavy cream

¼ cup (60 g) cream cheese

1–2 tablespoons (15 to 30 g) freshly grated horseradish

2 tablespoons (6 g) minced chives

Kosher salt to taste

Freshly ground black pepper to taste

FOR THE CRISPY CAPERS:

1 jar (3.5 ounces, or 99 g) capers, drained

Avocado oil or other neutral oil, for frying

FOR THE PIZZA:

1 Artisan Pizza Dough ball (see p. 35)

1 egg, beaten

3 tablespoons (36 g) everything bagel seasoning, plus more for serving

¼ cup (29 g) thinly sliced red onion

4 ounces (115 g) smoked salmon

1 tablespoon Pickled Shallots, drained (see p. 88)

1 ounce (28 g) black caviar (optional)

T his is my take on Wolfgang Puck's legendary pizza. His signature smoked salmon pizza at Spago helped define California-style pizza. Here, I update it with the kick of a horseradish-and-chive cream on an everything bagel seasoned crust. The crust gets an egg wash for the signature shine that makes a bagel so enticing. Finished with crispy capers and pickled shallots, it's an epic California pizza experience.

1 **To make the Horseradish-and-Chive Cream:** Combine the heavy cream and cream cheese in a bowl and whisk well to combine. The mixture should be thick but easily spreadable with a spoon. If it's too thin, continue whisking until thick. Fold in the horseradish and chives. Season to taste with kosher salt and black pepper. Set aside until ready to top the pizza. The Horseradish-and-Chive Cream Cream can be stored in an airtight container in the refrigerator for 3 to 4 days.

2 **To make the Crispy Capers:** Dry the drained capers on a plate lined with a few paper towels. Add enough oil to cover the capers to a small saucepan and bring to 350°F (180°C). Working in batches, fry the capers till golden brown, 2 to 3 minutes. Remove using a slotted spoon and transfer to a paper towel–lined plate to drain and cool. Set aside until ready to top the pizza. The Crispy Capers can be stored in an airtight container at room temperature for a few days.

3 **To make the pizza:** Preheat your indoor pizza oven with the temperature set to 700°F (370°C). When fully heated, set the heat balance dial (if equipped) to Bottom 3/Top 7. ➤➤

YIELD:
One 10-inch
(25-cm) to 12-inch
(30-cm) pizza

4 Stretch your pizza dough to 10 to 12 inches (25 to 30 cm) (see stretching techniques p. 10). Using a pastry brush, brush the outer rim of the crust (about an inch [2.5 cm] from the edge) with the beaten egg. Using the palm of your hand to prevent the 3 tablespoons (36 g) everything bagel seasoning from scattering everywhere, cradle the outside of the crust while you apply it to the washed portion of the dough.

5 Using a spoon, top the pizza with about ¼ cup of the Horseradish-and-Chive Cream. Save the rest for another pizza. Use the back of the spoon to spread it out evenly, leaving the crust bare. Scatter the red onions over the cream.

6 Check the temperature of the baking stone. It should be around 700°F to 750°F (370°C to 399°C) when loading the pizza into the oven. Slide the pizza onto the center of the baking stone and bake for about 5 minutes, turning a few times with a turning peel for an even bake. Keep an eye on the top of the pizza. You don't want the cream to burn. Adjust the balance dial if the sauce is getting dark.

7 When fully baked, the bottom of crust should be browned and dark in some spots. The top of the crust should be golden brown and the onions wilted from the heat. Remove the pizza from the oven using a turning peel and transfer to a wire rack to let the crust set for about 1 minute.

8 Transfer the pizza to a wooden peel to slice into 6 or 8 slices and slide the pizza onto your serving tray or plate. Top each slice with smoked salmon, Pickled Shallots, and a dollop of caviar (optional). Shower the pizza with about 1 tablespoon (9 g, save the rest for later) Crispy Capers and a sprinkle of everything bagel seasoning. Serve immediately.

BACON-TOMATO-AVOCADO PIZZA
WITH HEMP-HEART CRUST

1 Artisan Pizza Dough ball (see p. 35)

2 tablespoons (28 ml) avocado oil or other neutral oil

3 tablespoons (28 g) hemp hearts (shelled hemp seeds), plus more for serving

½ cup (125 g) cherry tomatoes, halved crosswise

2 slices uncooked bacon (2 ounces [55 g]), cut into lardons, par-cooked

⅓ cup (8 g) fresh basil leaves

1 small avocado, cut into 6–8 slices

Kosher salt to taste

Freshly ground black pepper to taste

YIELD:
One 10-inch (25-cm) to 12-inch (30-cm) pizza

Avocado? Hemp seeds? On a pizza? Can it get any more Californian? Honestly, probably. Don't make me push it any further—just try this pizza!

1 Preheat your indoor pizza oven with the temperature set to 700°F (370°C). When fully heated, set the heat balance dial (if equipped) to Bottom 3/Top 7.

2 Stretch your pizza dough to 10 to 12 inches (25 to 30 cm) (see stretching techniques p. 10). Using a pastry brush, brush the outer rim of the crust (about an inch [2.5 cm] from the edge) with the avocado oil. Take care to not drip too much excess oil onto your pizza peel.

3 Use the palm of your hand to cradle the outside of the crust while you apply the 3 tablespoons (28 g) of hemp seeds to the oiled portion of the dough. This trick helps the seeds adhere to the dough and prevent the seeds from getting everywhere (they still might). Top the pizza with the cherry tomatoes followed by the bacon.

4 Check the temperature of the baking stone. It should be around 700°F to 750°F (370°C to 399°C) when loading the pizza into the oven. Slide the pizza onto the center of the baking stone and bake for 4 to 5 minutes, turning a few times with a turning peel for an even bake. This pizza is more lightly topped than some. It may bake a little faster than other pizzas recipes in this chapter, so keep an eye on it. ➡

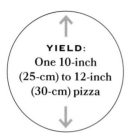

YIELD:
One 10-inch
(25-cm) to 12-inch
(30-cm) pizza

5 The pizza is done when the bottom is browned and dark in a few spots and the top of the crust is golden brown with lots of micro-blisters of varying toasty brown hues. The bacon should have rendered some of its fat and crisped up in places.

6 Remove the pizza from the oven using a turning peel and transfer to a wire rack to let the crust set for about 1 minute.

7 Transfer the pizza to a wooden peel to slice into 6 or 8 slices and slide the pizza onto your serving tray or plate. Tear the basil leaves directly onto the finished pizza. Place one slice of avocado on each slice and season with kosher salt and black pepper to taste. Sprinkle a generous pinch of hemp hearts over the pizza and serve immediately.

PEAR AND BLUE CHEESE PIZZA
WITH SPICED WALNUTS

FOR THE SPICED WALNUTS:

½ cup (50 g) walnuts

1 teaspoon maple syrup

1 teaspoon avocado or other neutral flavored oil

¼ teaspoon smoked paprika

¼ teaspoon kosher salt

Freshly ground black pepper to taste

FOR THE PIZZA:

1 Artisan Pizza Dough ball (see p. 35)

3 ounces (85 g) fresh mozzarella

⅓ cup (40 g) crumbled Roquefort or other strong blue cheese

½ teaspoon fresh thyme, leaves only, plus more for serving

1 Bosc pear, thinly sliced

1 tablespoon (15 ml) extra-virgin olive oil

Sea salt, to taste

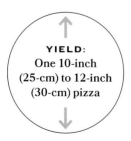

YIELD:
One 10-inch (25-cm) to 12-inch (30-cm) pizza

P ears, walnuts, and funky blue cheese have always been fast friends. Getting them together on a pizza is no exception. This pizza feels nice and cozy as part of a holiday spread and goes perfect with a leafy green salad topped with sliced pears dressed in a tangy vinaigrette.

1 **To make the Spiced Walnuts:** Preheat a home oven to 300°F (150°C, or gas mark 2). Combine the walnuts, maple syrup, oil, and seasonings to a small bowl and toss well. Roast on a parchment-lined baking sheet, 8 to 10 minutes, being careful not to burn. Let cool completely before topping pizza or storing. Spiced Walnuts can be stored in an airtight container at room temperature for 1 to 2 weeks or longer in the refrigerator or freezer.

2 **To make the pizza:** Preheat your indoor pizza oven with the temperature set to 700°F (370°C). When fully heated, set the heat balance dial (if equipped) to Bottom 3/Top 7.

3 Stretch your pizza dough to 10 to 12 inches (25 to 30 cm) (see stretching techniques p. 10). Leaving room for the crust to rise, scatter the fresh mozzarella over the top of the pizza, breaking it up with your hands as you go. Top with the blue cheese, thyme leaves, and pear slices. Drizzle with olive oil.

4 Check the temperature of the baking stone. It should be around 700°F to 750°F (370°C to 399°C) when loading the pizza into the oven. Slide the pizza onto the center of the baking stone and bake for 4 to 5 minutes, turning the pizza a few times with a turning peel for an even bake.

5 When the bottom of the pizza is golden brown with a few dark spots and the micro-blisters of the crust have darkened, but not burned, remove the pizza from the oven and transfer to a wire rack and shower with the Spiced Walnuts. Let the crust set for about 1 minute on the rack.

6 Transfer the pizza to a wooden peel to slice and slide the pizza onto your serving tray or plate. Sprinkle the finished pizza with a pinch of sea salt and some additional fresh thyme leaves. Serve immediately.

STUFFED MUSHROOM
PIZZA

FOR THE STUFFED MUSHROOMS:

2 slices bacon, diced

½ pound (225 g) sweet Italian sausage (or homemade Fennel Sausage see p. 67), casing removed

1 clove garlic, minced

1 shallot, minced

¼ teaspoon red chili flakes (optional)

1 teaspoon sherry vinegar

½ teaspoon fresh thyme

1 tablespoon (4 g) chopped parsley

2 ounces (55 g) cream cheese, softened

¼ cup (25 g) finely shredded Parmigiano Reggiano

¼ cup (28 g) panko breadcrumbs

Kosher salt to taste

Freshly ground black pepper to taste

12 cremini or baby bella mushrooms, stems removed

The dinner party appetizer staple, but this time, it's pizza! Savory stuffed mushrooms filled with sausage and bacon are nested on a pizza topped with creamy fontina cheese. This is rich and rib-sticking pizza.

1 **To make the Stuffed Mushrooms:** Heat a large skillet over medium heat. Add the bacon and sausage. Cook, stirring often until the sausage is browned and the bacon begins to crisp. Use a slotted spoon to transfer the bacon and sausage to a bowl, reserving about a tablespoon (15 ml) of rendered fat in the pan. Reduce the heat to low, add the garlic and shallot, and cook stirring often, till just softened. Add the chili flakes (optional) and deglaze the pan with the sherry vinegar, scraping any bits that are stuck to the pan. Transfer the mixture to the bowl with the bacon and sausage. Let cool. Add the thyme, parsley, cream cheese, Parmigiano Reggiano, and breadcrumbs to the bowl and fold to combine. Season to taste with kosher salt and black pepper. Stuff the mixture into the mushrooms. Set aside till ready to top the pizza. The prepped Stuffed Mushrooms can be stored in an airtight container in the refrigerator for 1 to 2 days.

2 **To make the pizza:** Preheat your indoor pizza oven with the temperature set to 650°F (343°C). When fully heated, set the heat balance dial (if equipped) to Bottom 3/Top 7.

3 Mix the shredded cheeses in a bowl and set aside. Stretch your pizza dough to 10 to 12 inches (25 to 30 cm) (see stretching techniques p. 10). Top the pizza with the shredded cheese mixture, leaving room for the crust to rise. Place one Stuffed Mushroom in the center of the pizza and 4 to 5 around it in a circle. Place the remaining Stuffed Mushrooms along the edge of the

FOR THE PIZZA:

1 Artisan Pizza Dough ball
(see p. 35)

2 ounces (55 g) fontina
cheese, thickly shredded

2 ounces (55 g) low-
moisture whole-milk
mozzarella cheese, thickly
shredded

¼ cup (28 g) panko bread-
crumbs

Kosher salt to taste

Freshly ground black
pepper to taste

¼ cup (25 g) finely shredded
Parmigiano Reggiano

Small handful fresh basil

¼ teaspoon fresh thyme

¼ teaspoon minced fresh
parsley

crust. Push the mushrooms into the crust gently to prevent them from moving around too much when transferring the pizza to the oven. Sprinkle the panko breadcrumbs over the top of the pizza and season with a pinch of kosher salt and a few cranks of freshly ground black pepper.

4 Check the temperature of the baking stone. It should be around 600°F to 650°F (316°C to 343°C) when loading the pizza into the oven. Slide the pizza onto the center of the baking stone and bake for 4 to 5 minutes, turning the pizza a few times with a turning peel for an even bake.

5 The pizza is done when the bottom is browned and dark in a few spots and the top of the crust is golden brown. The mushrooms should have softened and cooked through. If not, return the pizza to the oven to bake longer, adjusting the balance dial to prevent the bottom of the crust from burning.

6 Remove the pizza from the oven using a turning peel and transfer to a wire rack to let the crust set for about 1 minute.

7 Transfer the pizza to a wooden peel to slice into 6 or 8 slices and slide the pizza onto your serving tray or plate. Shower the pizza with Parmigiano Reggiano, tear the basil leaves directly onto the pizza, and sprinkle with remaining fresh herbs. Serve immediately.

Note: This pizza bakes at a lower temperature than other pizza recipes in this chapter. The low temperature and extended baking time allows the stuffed mushrooms to fully cook.

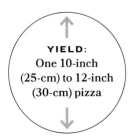

YIELD:
One 10-inch
(25-cm) to 12-inch
(30-cm) pizza

Chapter 3
Thin and Crispy Pizzas

Cracker-thin, crispy pizza baked directly on the oven stone. Often called Chicago tavern-style pizza, this pizza differs from "bar-style," which is baked in a pan. It's the "real Chicago pizza" according to most Chicagoans. The heat of the stone puffs up the super thin crust into a crispy, crunchy crust that can hold a wealth of toppings but isn't dry.

Thin and crispy pizza is an easy bake in an indoor pizza oven. The consistent heat makes the experience less stressful than other ovens and helps ensure a crackly crisp bottom. This style takes the sauce and toppings pretty much all the way to the edge of the crust. Use caution when topping, you don't want them to spill over the edge of the crust and on to the baking stone. A pizza spilling toppings on to a hot baking surface will generate a ton of unpleasant smoke. If this happens, make sure that you don't unplug the oven after you finish baking the pizza and turn the oven off. The better oven models contain filtration systems that will filter the smoke even after being turned off, preventing the smoke from all spilling out into your house.

EQUIPMENT AND TOOLS
WOODEN ROLLING PIN

A wooden rolling pin works well at rolling out thin and crispy pizza. It's not uncommon to see this style of pizza dough being prepared with a "dough-sheeter," a commercial baking tool used to quickly stretch super thin pizzas. At home, a rolling pin is the most reasonable, next best thing.

PIZZA TRAYS FOR PROOFING

The thin and crispy pizza dough is best after being rolled out, shaped, and left to cold proof. Metal pizza trays lined with parchment paper are what I use at home.

WOODEN PIZZA PEEL

For the thin and crispy pizzas, I like to build and top my pizzas on a wooden pizza peel. A wooden peel lightly dusted with flour should allow a fully topped pizza to slide right off and into the oven. Metal pizza peels can stick easily and should be reserved for quickly transferring pizzas, not stretching and building them.

PIZZA TURNING PEEL

A pizza turning peel is the best tool for turning and maneuvering thin and crispy pizza as it bakes. The turning peel keeps the pizza in the oven and in contact with the baking surface while turning. This result is a better baked pizza.

ROLLER PIZZA CUTTER

I slice my round pizzas with a classic, wheel-style pizza cutter. A high-quality cutter should produce clean-cut slices with little drag.

PIZZA SCREEN FOR SERVING

I serve my pizza on a pizza screen nested in a pizza tray to keep it crisp while serving. Slice the pizza on a cutting board before transferring.

THIN AND CRISPY PIZZA
DOUGH

155 grams filtered water

7 grams kosher salt

1.5 grams instant dry yeast

225 grams bread flour

15 grams ground semolina flour, plus more as needed

1–2 teaspoons (5–10 ml) avocado oil or other neutral-flavored oil

Rice flour as needed

YIELD:
Two dough balls for two 10-inch (25-cm) to 12-inch (30-cm) pizzas

This makes a cracker-thin pizza dough with a light and airy crunch. The dough can be rolled super thin but is sturdy enough to bake directly on the baking stone. It puffs and crisps up beautifully thanks to this direct contact with the fully heated oven deck. This is my take on the famous Chicago "tavern-style" pizza dough, made easily at home with an indoor pizza oven.

1 Pour the filtered water into a large mixing bowl, add the salt, and stir to dissolve completely. Sprinkle the dry yeast onto the surface of the water and let the yeast absorb some of the water briefly for about 1 minute before stirring to dissolve completely. Add both flours.

2 Using your hands, mix the ingredients, stirring and pinching with your fingers till all the ingredients are fully incorporated and no dry flour remains. Cover and let rest at room temperature (about 70°F [21°C]) for 20 minutes.

3 After 20 minutes, uncover the dough and knead for 2 to 3 minutes directly in the bowl or on a work surface till mostly smooth. Cover and let rest at room temperature (about 70°F [21°C]) for 1 hour.

4 After 1 hour, uncover the bowl and lightly knead the dough using your hands. Cover the dough while you prepare the dough tray, bowls, or plates. Lightly coat your dough tray, plates, or bowls, with a thin layer of oil. It should be nicely slicked, but not pooled. Remove any excess oil with a paper towel.

5 Uncover the dough and transfer to a work surface. Knead the dough a couple times and form into a ball. Using a bench scraper, divide the dough into 2 equal portions (I use a scale for this). ➤➤

Form each portion into a dough ball by folding the edges of the dough into the center and repeating the process a few times until the tops of the dough balls are smooth. Pinch the dough balls closed with your fingers and place on your work surface. Give each dough ball a couple spins with your hands to smooth out the bottom a bit.

6   Transfer the dough balls to the oiled dough tray, bowls, or plates. Using a pastry brush, brush a thin coat of oil on the surface of each dough ball. Cover and transfer to the refrigerator to cold ferment for 24 hours.

7   After 24 hours, remove the container of dough from the refrigerator and let rest at room temperature (about 70°F [21°C]) for about 30 minutes or till it no longer feels cold to the touch. Dust a large work surface with semolina. Transfer a dough ball to the floured work surface and flatten using your hand. Dust a rolling pin with semolina and roll the dough ball out into a 12-inch (30 cm) circle, avoiding the center at first so it doesn't get too thin.

8   The bottom of the dough should be well dusted with semolina and shouldn't be sticky.

9   Carefully transfer the rolled-out dough to a parchment paper–lined sheet pan or pizza tray that has been dusted with rice flour and semolina. Place a piece of parchment paper over the dough and repeat the process with the remaining dough ball. Wrap the parchment-covered dough in plastic wrap to prevent it from drying it out and transfer to the refrigerator to cure for at least 6 hours or up to 72 hours. Remove the dough from the refrigerator to bring to room temperature before using.

THIN AND CRISPY PIZZA
SAUCE

1 jar (19.7 ounces, or
560 grams) tomato puree

¼ cup (65 g) tomato paste

2 teaspoons dried oregano

1 teaspoon garlic powder

Kosher salt to taste

For pizza this thin, it's wise not to use a watery sauce. It soaks right through the cracker-thin pizza shells. I opt for thicker tomato puree over crushed tomatoes to build my Thin and Crispy Pizza Sauce base. It keeps things extra crispy.

1 Add the tomatoes, oregano, and garlic to a 1-quart (946 ml) deli container. Blend with an immersion blender until smooth.

2 Season to taste with kosher salt. The thin and crispy pizza sauce can be stored in an airtight container in the refrigerator for up to a week.

YIELD:
About 1½ cups
(355 ml)

CHICAGO-STYLE TAVERN PIZZA
WITH PARMESAN-DUSTED HOMEMADE FENNEL SAUSAGE

FOR THE FENNEL SAUSAGE:

2 pounds (910 g) coarsely ground pork, 20–25% fat

20 grams fennel seeds, lightly toasted

15 grams kosher salt

1 teaspoon sugar

1 teaspoon garlic powder

½ teaspoon dried oregano

1 teaspoon freshly ground black pepper

FOR THE PIZZA:

3 ounces (85 g) low-moisture whole-milk mozzarella cheese, thickly shredded

3 ounces (85 g) low-moisture part-skim mozzarella cheese, thickly shredded

1 Thin and Crispy Pizza Dough ball, rolled out and fully proofed (see p. 63)

5 ounces (150 ml) Thin and Crispy Pizza Sauce (see p. 65)

½ cup (50 g) finely shredded Parmigiano Reggiano

Homemade fennel sausage is the star of what Chicago locals call "real Chicago pizza." Chicago is a pizza town. It's also a sausage town. Pizzerias pride themselves on using fresh, locally made Italian sausage. It's the topping of choice, and it's applied liberally. Making it yourself is the way to go, and it's easier than you think. Sure, you can grind the pork shoulder at home, but you can also head to your local butcher counter ask them to coarsely grind a couple pounds (910 g) for you. The fresh pork along with the toasty fennel will make "extra-sausage" your standard.

1   **To make the Fennel Sausage:** Combine the ground pork, fennel seeds, salt, sugar, garlic powder, oregano, and black pepper in a bowl. Mix very well. Transfer to an airtight container and keep chilled until ready to top the pizza. The Fennel Sausage can be stored in an airtight container in the refrigerator for 1 to 2 days or frozen for up to 2 months.

2   **To make the pizza:** Preheat your indoor pizza oven with the temperature set to 650°F (343°C). When fully heated, set the heat balance dial (if equipped) to Bottom 4/Top 6.

3   Combine the whole-milk and part-skim milk mozzarella cheeses in a bowl. Set aside until ready to top the pizza.

4   Transfer the pizza dough shell to a wooden pizza peel dusted with semolina. Ladle the sauce into the center of the pizza and spread it out towards the crust in a circular motion using the back of the ladle, leaving about ¼-inch (0.6 cm) of the outer crust bare. Top the pizza with 8 ounces (225 g) of sausage, forming the bulk sausage into loose balls about the size of a marble with your hands. ➤➤

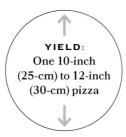

YIELD:
One 10-inch
(25-cm) to 12-inch
(30-cm) pizza

Roll the balls of sausage in the Parmigiano Reggiano before placing on the pizza. You should end up with about 18 pieces of sausage on the fully topped pizza. Scatter the blend of mozzarella cheese over the sausage.

5 Check the temperature of the baking stone. It should be around 600°F to 650°F (316°C to 343°C) when loading the pizza into the oven. Slide the pizza onto the center of the baking stone and bake for 6 to 8 minutes, turning the pizza a few times with a turning peel for an even bake.

6 Look for the bottom of the crust to be golden brown and dark in some spots. It should feel set and crisp when picked up with the turning peel.

7 When fully baked, remove the pizza from the oven using a turning peel and transfer to a wire rack to let the crust set for about 1 minute.

8 Transfer the pizza to a wooden peel to slice into squares, "party cut" style, and slide the pizza onto your serving tray or plate. Serve immediately.

MUSHROOM UMAMI BOMB
PIZZA

FOR THE ROASTED PORTABELLA MUSHROOMS:

3–4 portabella mushrooms, stems removed and cleaned of dark gills

2 tablespoons (32 g) white miso paste

2 tablespoons (28 ml) avocado oil or neutral oil

1 tablespoon (9 g) coconut sugar or (15 g) brown sugar

1 tablespoon (15 ml) maple syrup

1 small lemon, juice and zest

FOR THE SPICY SHIITAKE MUSHROOMS:

1 teaspoon soy sauce

1 teaspoon sesame oil

1 teaspoon gochujang

½ teaspoon coconut sugar or brown sugar

⅓ cup (80 ml) water

5 ounces (140 g) sliced shitake mushrooms

➥➥

YIELD:
One 10-inch (25-cm) to 12-inch (30-cm) pizza

An umami-packed flavor bomb of a pizza that just happens to be vegan. The earthy, savory flavor of mushrooms prepared two ways is bumped up to levels that make any meat or dairy feel like overkill. The mushroom-covered pizza gets piled post-bake with wild arugula dressed in a tangy Miso-Maple Dressing. Get your taste buds ready to tingle.

1 **To make the Roasted Portabella Mushrooms (24 hours before baking pizza):** Place the mushrooms in a shallow baking dish. Combine the white miso, oil, sugar, maple syrup, and the lemon juice and zest in a bowl. Whisk to dissolve the sugar and combine. Pour the marinade over the mushrooms, making sure to cover all the surfaces for maximum flavor. Cover and transfer to the refrigerator overnight or for at least 4 hours. After marinating the mushrooms, heat a home over to 350°F (180°C, or gas mark 4) with the rack in the middle position. Drain the mushrooms and transfer to a foil-lined baking sheet. Roast, gill-side down, until tender, 20 to 25 minutes. Let cool before slicing and topping pizza. The Roasted Portabella Mushrooms can be stored in an airtight container in the refrigerator for 3 to 4 days.

2 **To make the Spicy Shiitake Mushrooms:** Combine the soy sauce, sesame oil, gochujang, and sugar in a small bowl and whisk to combine. Set aside. Heat a sauté pan over medium-high heat. Add the water and mushrooms. Cook until the mushrooms have softened, about 3 minutes. Reduce the heat to low and add the sauce, stir to coat, and cook, stirring often till the mushrooms begin to caramelize, 7 to 8 minutes. Transfer to a bowl to cool before topping the pizza. The Spicy Shitake Mushrooms can be stored in an airtight container in the refrigerator for 3 to 4 days. ➥➥

MUSHROOM UMAMI BOMB PIZZA, CONT.

3 **To make the Miso-Maple Dressing:** Combine the sesame oil, maple syrup, white miso, and lemon juice and zest in a small bowl and whisk to combine. Set aside. The Miso-Maple Dressing can be stored in an airtight container in the refrigerator for up to a week.

4 **To make the pizza:** Preheat your indoor pizza oven with the temperature set to 650°F (343°C). When fully heated, set the heat balance dial (if equipped) to Bottom 4/Top 6.

5 Transfer the pizza dough shell to a wooden pizza peel dusted with semolina. Sprinkle the sesame seeds all over the top, pushing them in gently with your fingers.

6 Spread the Spicy Shiitake Mushrooms all over the pizza and top with the Roasted Portabella Mushrooms.

7 Check the temperature of the baking stone. It should be around 600°F to 650°F (316°C to 343°C) when loading the pizza into the oven. Slide the pizza onto the center of the baking stone and bake for 6 to 8 minutes, turning the pizza a few times with a turning peel for an even bake.

8 Look for the bottom of the crust to be golden brown and dark in some spots. It should feel set and cracker-crisp when picked up with the turning peel.

9 When fully baked, remove the pizza from the oven using a turning peel and transfer to a wire rack to let the crust set for about 1 minute.

10 Toss the arugula with the Miso-Maple Dressing in a bowl.

11 Transfer the pizza to a wooden peel to slice and slide the pizza onto your serving tray or plate. Pile the dressed arugula in the center of the pizza and sprinkle with additional sesame seeds. Serve immediately.

Note: For the Mushroom Umami Bomb Pizza, dust the top of the dough heavily with sesame seeds as you roll it out.

SAUSAGE AND CHICAGO-STYLE GIARDINIERA
PIZZA

3 ounces (85 g) low-moisture whole-milk mozzarella cheese, thickly shredded

3 ounces (85 g) low-moisture part-skim mozzarella cheese, thickly shredded

1 Thin and Crispy Pizza Dough ball, rolled out and fully proofed (see p. 63)

5 ounces (150 ml) Thin and Crispy Pizza Sauce (see p. 65)

¼ cup (52 g) Chicago-style giardiniera, plus more for serving

8 ounces (225 g) home-made Fennel Sausage (see p. 67)

YIELD:
One 10-inch (25-cm) to 12-inch (30-cm) pizza

This is a Windy City classic combo. The briny bite of Chicago-style giardiniera pairs perfectly with rich, homemade sausage. While often composed of the same ingredients, Chicago-style giardiniera differs from the more common Italian-style giardiniera by swapping out the vinegar for oil after pickling. Additionally, the mixture is chopped into something more like a relish. Some versions pack the heat thanks to the addition of hot peppers. It's a perfect topping for thin and crispy tavern-style pizzas.

1 Preheat your indoor pizza oven with the temperature set to 650°F (343°C). When fully heated, set the heat balance dial (if equipped) to Bottom 4/Top 6.

2 Combine the whole-milk and part-skim milk mozzarella cheeses in a bowl. Set aside until ready to top the pizza. Ladle the sauce into the center of the pizza and spread it out toward the crust in a circular motion using the back of the ladle, leaving about ¼-inch (0.6 cm) of the outer crust bare. Scatter the blend of mozzarella cheese all over the top of the sauce, followed by the Chicago-style giardiniera. Apply the sausage in large marble-size sausage chunks, about 18 chunks total.

3 Check the temperature of the baking stone. It should be around 600°F to 650°F (316°C to 343°C) when loading the pizza into the oven. Slide the pizza onto the center of the baking stone and bake for 6 to 8 minutes, turning the pizza a few times with a turning peel for an even bake.

4 Look for the bottom of the crust to be golden brown and dark in some spots. It should feel set and crisp when picked up with the turning peel.

5 When fully baked, remove the pizza from the oven using a turning peel and transfer to a wire rack to let the crust set for about 1 minute.

6 Transfer the pizza to a wooden peel to slice into squares, "party cut" style, and slide the pizza onto your serving tray or plate. Serve immediately with additional Chicago-style giardiniera on the side for spooning on slices to taste.

Note: Don't substitute with Italian-style giardiniera. It's significantly different. It's worth seeking out or ordering real Chicago-style giardiniera.

THIN AND CRISPY PIZZAS

TACO
TAVERN PIZZA

FOR THE TACO MEAT TOPPING:

½ pound (225 g) ground beef

2 teaspoons taco seasoning

¼ cup (60 ml) tomato sauce

FOR THE PIZZA:

3 ounces (85 g) pepper jack cheese, thickly shredded

3 ounces (85 g) low-moisture part-skim mozzarella

1 Thin and Crispy Pizza Dough ball, rolled out and fully proofed (see p. 63)

¼ cup (60 ml) red enchilada sauce

½ cup (130 g) refried beans

½ cup (120 g) salsa fresca or pico de gallo, divided

2 cups (144 g) shredded iceberg lettuce or (94 g) romaine lettuce

2–3 green onions, sliced

¼ cup (60 g) sour cream

Hot sauce or chili-based salsa

Crispy, crunchy, and tortilla-thin, my Thin and Crispy Pizza Dough is perfect for the ultimate in taco pizzas. This pizza is absolutely loaded with taco night flavors, stacked high. It's a mess to eat in the best way.

1 **To make the Taco Meat Topping:** Heat a large skillet over medium-high heat and add the ground beef. Break up any large chunks of beef (I find a potato masher to be excellent for this) and add the taco seasoning. Cook till browned, 5 to 7 minutes. Add the tomato sauce and cook over medium-high heat till the tomato sauce clings to the beef and is mostly reduced, 2 to 3 minutes. Let cool fully before topping pizza. The Taco Meat Topping can be stored in an airtight container in the refrigerator for 3 to 4 days.

2 **To make the pizza:** Preheat your indoor pizza oven with the temperature set to 650°F (343°C). When fully heated, set the heat balance dial (if equipped) to Bottom 4/Top 6.

3 Combine the pepper jack cheese and mozzarella cheese in a bowl and set aside until ready to top the pizza. Transfer the pizza dough shell to a wooden pizza peel dusted with semolina. Spread the enchilada sauce all over the pizza dough. You want the sauce close to the edge of the dough for this style pizza, but leave about ¼-inch (0.6 cm) bare to prevent the sauce from spilling onto the baking stone. Add dollops of the refried beans all over the sauce and top with the shredded cheese mixture. Scatter about ½ cup (115 g) of the Taco Meat Topping over the top, along with half of the salsa fresca.

4 Check the temperature of the baking stone. It should be around 600°F to 650°F (316°C to 343°C) when loading the pizza into the oven. Slide the pizza onto the center of the baking stone and bake

for 6 to 8 minutes, turning the pizza a few times with a turning peel for an even bake. Look for the bottom of the crust to be golden brown and dark in some spots. It should feel set and crisp when picked up with the turning peel.

5 When fully baked, remove the pizza from the oven using a turning peel and transfer to a wire rack to let the crust set for about 1 minute.

6 Transfer the pizza to a wooden peel to slice and slide the pizza onto your serving tray or plate. Top the finished pizza with the shredded lettuce, followed by the remaining salsa fresca and green onions. Top each slice with a spoonful of sour cream and drizzle the entire pizza with hot sauce. Serve immediately.

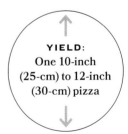

YIELD:
One 10-inch
(25-cm) to 12-inch
(30-cm) pizza

Chapter 4
Neapolitan-Style Pizzas

This is *the* original pizza. Built on tradition and experience, Neapolitan-style pizza is often a hyper-focused affair composed of minimal ingredients treated in very specific ways to bring out their best. Baked quickly and with high heat, the integrity of more delicate ingredients is better preserved in the finished slice than some other pizzas styles.

It's remarkable that pizza oven technology has advanced enough to be able to produce Neapolitan-style pizza indoors successfully without an open flame or elaborate oven installations. The best models of indoor pizza ovens deliver enough heat high to make authentic Neapolitan-style pizza that looks like it came straight out of a traditional wood-fired oven.

EQUIPMENT AND TOOLS

STONE WORK SURFACE

I stretch and top my Neapolitan-style pizza on a traditional marble surface and then transfer it to the oven on a metal peel. A stone work surface such as marble helps regulate the temperature of the dough as you work it. This keeps the dough from becoming sticky and allows the pizza maker to use less flour when stretching.

PERFORATED METAL PIZZA PEEL

Traditional, Neapolitan-style pizza is most often stretched and built on a work surface and then quickly transferred to a metal pizza peel for loading into the oven. The raw dough doesn't spend much time on the metal surface, making sticking less of a concern. I prefer the perforated styles as they help shed any excess flour from the bottom of the pizza and prevent oven flare-ups.

PIZZA TURNING PEEL

A pizza turning peel is the traditional tool for turning and handling Neapolitan pizza as it bakes. The turning peel keeps the pizza in the oven and in contact with the baking surface while turning. This result is a better baked pizza.

ROLLER PIZZA CUTTER OR PIZZA SCISSORS

I slice my round pizzas with a classic, wheel-style pizza cutter. A high-quality cutter should produce clean-cut slices with little drag. Pizza scissors are traditional for Neapolitan-style pizza, but not required.

PIZZA SCREEN AND TRAY FOR SERVING

I serve my pizza on a pizza screen nested in a pizza tray to keep it crisp while serving. Slice the pizza on a cutting board before transferring.

NEAPOLITAN-STYLE
PIZZA DOUGH

200 grams filtered water

10 grams kosher salt

1 gram instant dry yeast

315 grams Caputo "00" Pizzeria Flour (In the blue and white bag, not the red bag; that's "Chef's Flour")

Olive oil, for brushing the dough tray

A traditional Neapolitan-style pizza dough for making authentic Neapolitan pizza at home. Neapolitan pizza dough is composed of a simple combination of flour, water, and yeast. The flour here is especially important. Double-zero, or "00," flour is designed specifically for the high heat and quick-baking times required for authentic Neapolitan-style pizza. Look for Caputo "00" Pizzeria Flour in the blue and white bag for best results.

1 **At least 8 hours before baking pizza or preferably (cold fermented) 18 to 72 hours before:** Pour the filtered water into a large mixing bowl, add the salt, and stir to dissolve completely. Sprinkle the yeast on the surface of the water and let the yeast absorb some of the water for about 1 minute before stirring to dissolve completely. Add the flour.

2 Using your hands, mix the ingredients, stirring and pinching with your fingers till all the ingredients are fully incorporated and no dry flour remains. Do not knead at this point. Cover and let rest at room temperature (about 70°F [21°C]) for 20 to 30 minutes. This rest gives the flour some time to absorb the water and makes the dough easier to knead.

3 After 20 to 30 minutes, uncover the dough and knead for 2 to 3 minutes directly in the bowl or on a work surface till mostly smooth. Cover and let rest at room temperature (about 70°F [21°C]) for 1 to 2 hours.

4 After 1 hour, the dough should have risen some and look mostly shiny. Uncover the dough and pick up the dough ball. It should feel lighter now, like it has some air in it. Knead the dough in the bowl using your hands, de-gassing any large bubbles that may have formed. Cover and let rest for about 30 minutes. ➻

YIELD:
2 pizza dough balls for two 10-inch (25-cm) to 12-inch (30-cm) pizzas

5 Uncover and lightly knead the dough in the bowl using your hands. Cover the dough while you prepare the dough tray, bowls, or plates.

6 Lightly coat your dough tray, plates, or bowls with a thin layer of oil. It should be nicely slicked, but not pooled. Remove any excess oil with a paper towel.

7 Uncover the dough and transfer to a work surface. Knead the dough a couple times and form into a large ball. Using a bench scraper, divide the dough into 2 equal portions (I use a scale for this). Form each portion into a dough ball by folding the edges of the dough into the center and repeating the process a few times until the tops of the dough balls are smooth. Pinch the dough balls closed with your fingers and place on your work surface. Give each dough ball a couple spins with your hands to smooth out the bottom a bit.

8 Transfer the dough balls to the oiled dough tray, bowls, or plates. Cover and transfer to the refrigerator to cold ferment for 18 to 72 hours. If using the dough the same day, cover but do not refrigerate and proceed with the next steps.

9 **4 to 6 hours before baking the pizzas:** Remove the dough tray, bowls, or plates from the refrigerator and let the dough rise, covered, at room temperature (about 70°F [21°C]) for 4 to 6 hours before stretching and baking. Look for the dough to have expanded and risen with lots of small bubbles on the surface.

NEAPOLITAN-STYLE RUSTIC
RED SAUCE

1 can (28 ounces, or 785 ml) whole peeled tomatoes (high-quality San Marzano DOP tomatoes are traditional)

2 teaspoons kosher salt, or to taste

A simple, bright sauce for authentic Neapolitan-style pizza. For quick-baking Neapolitan-style pizza, I like to keep the tomato flavor fresh and forward. Seasoning with herbs can be a distraction. Instead, source the best canned tomatoes you can find and process them minimally. It's simple sauce at its best. I find a good blast of salt can really help awaken the tomatoes, so I go a little heavier here than I would with other sauces.

1 Empty the can of tomatoes into a colander positioned over a bowl to catch the juices, drain, and transfer the whole tomatoes to a bowl. Reserve the juices for another use. Season the tomatoes with the kosher salt and use your hands to crush the tomatoes into a chunky sauce. You want to break up large chunks so the sauce can be spread with a spoon.

2 Transfer to a 12-ounce (355 ml) deli container or lidded bowl. Prepared sauce can be stored in an airtight container in the refrigerator for up to week. Bring to room temperature before topping your pizza.

YIELD:
10 to 12 ounces
(285 to 355 ml)

PIZZA MARGHERITA

1 Neapolitan-Style Pizza Dough ball (see p. 79)

3 ounces (85 g) Neapolitan-Style Rustic Red Sauce (see p. 81)

Large handful fresh basil, divided

4 ounces (115 g) fresh mozzarella cheese pearls

2 tablespoons (28 ml) extra-virgin olive oil, divided

¼ teaspoon sea salt, or to taste

The classic of all classics, Pizza Margherita is a simple pizza. It's always a must. For this version, I include the basil in the bake as well as applying more fresh basil after it comes out of the oven. I don't mind being blasted by basil. It's pizza's perfect perfume. A sprinkle of sea salt just before serving helps pop this iconic pizza.

1 Preheat your indoor pizza oven with the temperature set to 850°F (454°C). When fully heated, set the heat balance dial (if equipped) to Bottom 0/Top 10.

2 Stretch your pizza dough to 10 to 12 inches (25 to 30 cm) (see stretching techniques p. 10). Ladle the sauce into the center of the pizza and spread it out toward the crust in a circular motion, leaving about 1½ inches (3.8 cm) of the outer crust bare. Reserve a few basil leaves to top the finished pizza and tear the rest directly onto the sauce. Scatter the mozzarella cheese pearls all over the pizza, leaving room for the sauce to still be visible after it melts. It should take about 15 small pieces of cheese. Drizzle with half of the olive oil.

3 Check the temperature of the baking stone. It should be around 800°F to 900°F (427°C to 482°C) when loading the pizza into the oven. Slide the pizza onto the center of the baking stone and bake for 1 to 2 minutes, turning once or twice with a turning peel for an even bake. If the bottom of the pizza is baking too quickly, adjust the balance dial. If the bottom becomes too blackened but the top needs additional time, lift the pizza off the baking stone using a turning peel and hold it close to the roof of the oven to quickly finish cooking the top. Use caution as you want the cheese to melt but not darken.

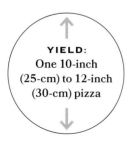

YIELD:
One 10-inch (25-cm) to 12-inch (30-cm) pizza

4 Look for the top and bottom of the crust to brown with lots of tiny dark spots, called *leopard spotting*, all over. The crust should feel set and not too floppy when picked up with a turning peel. When fully baked, remove the pizza from the oven and transfer to a wire rack to let the crust briefly set for about 30 seconds.

5 Transfer the pizza to a wooden peel to slice and slide the pizza onto your serving tray or plate. Tear the remaining basil leaves on to the finished pizza and drizzle with remaining olive oil. Sprinkle the pizza with a pinch of sea salt. Serve immediately.

RADICCHIO AND GOAT CHEESE PIZZA
WITH TANGERINE GASTRIQUE

FOR THE TANGERINE GASTRIQUE:

½ cup (96 g) cane sugar

½ cup (120 ml) sherry vinegar, plus more as needed

1–2 tangerines, juice and zest

Kosher salt to taste

Freshly ground black pepper to taste

FOR THE PIZZA:

1 Neapolitan-Style Pizza Dough ball (see p. 79)

2 ounces (55 g) fresh mozzarella cheese

2 ounces (55 g) goat cheese, crumbled

1 head radicchio, cut into thin strips

1 teaspoon fresh mint leaves

YIELD:
One 10-inch (25-cm) to 12-inch (30-cm) pizza

A citrusy, sweet, and sour gastrique balances the slightly bitter flavor of the Italian chicory on this Neapolitan-style pizza. The mound of radicchio collapses in the heat of the oven and on to a bed of tangy goat cheese and fresh mozzarella. A handful of fresh mint leaves to finish with the drizzle of tangerine gastrique has this pizza feeling fancy. The leftover gastrique from the recipe is delicious drizzled on roasted meats and vegetables or incorporated into salad dressings.

1   **To make the Tangerine Gastrique:** Combine the sugar, vinegar, and tangerine juice in a small saucepan and bring to a boil over high heat, reduce heat to medium-high, and cook, stirring often, until the sugar is completely dissolved, and sauce is reduced to a light, syrupy consistency, about 10 minutes. Stir in the zest. Let cool. Season to taste with kosher salt and black pepper. If the gastrique is too thick or sweet, whisk in additional sherry vinegar, 1 teaspoon at a time.

2   **To make the pizza:** Preheat your indoor pizza oven with the temperature set to 850°F (454°C). When fully heated, set the heat balance dial (if equipped) to Bottom 0/Top 10.

3   Stretch your pizza dough to 10 to 12 inches (25 to 30 cm) (see stretching techniques p. 10). Leaving room for the crust to rise, scatter the fresh mozzarella over the top of the pizza, breaking it up with your hands as you go. Top with the goat cheese and radicchio. Don't be alarmed if it looks like a ton of radicchio. It will cook down significantly in the oven.

4 Check the temperature of the baking stone. It should be around 800°F to 900°F (427°C to 482°C) when loading the pizza into the oven. Slide the pizza onto the center of the baking stone and bake for 1 to 2 minutes, turning once or twice with a turning peel for an even bake. If the bottom of the pizza is baking too quickly, adjust the balance dial. If the bottom becomes too blackened but the top needs additional time, lift the pizza off the baking stone using a turning peel and hold it close to the roof of the oven to quickly finish cooking the top.

5 Look for the top and bottom of the crust to brown with lots of tiny dark spots all over. The crust should feel set and not too floppy when picked up with a turning peel. When fully baked, remove the pizza from the oven and transfer to a wire rack to let the crust briefly set for about 30 seconds.

6 Transfer the pizza to a wooden peel to slice and slide the pizza onto your serving tray or plate. Tear the fresh mint leaves on to the finished pizza and drizzle with the Tangerine Gastrique. Serve immediately.

PISTACHIO PESTO PIZZA
WITH MORTADELLA AND ROBIOLA CHEESE

FOR THE PISTACHIO PESTO:

½ cup (62 g) pistachios

2 cloves garlic, minced

3 cups (72 g) packed basil leaves

1 small lemon, juice and zest

½–¾ cup (120 to 175 ml) extra-virgin olive oil, divided

½ cup (50 g) finely shredded Parmigiano Reggiano

Kosher salt to taste

Freshly ground black pepper to taste

FOR THE PIZZA:

1 Neapolitan-Style Pizza Dough ball (see p. 79)

4 ounces (115 g) Robiola cheese, cut into small chunks

5–6 slices (about ¼ pound [115 g]) mortadella

Small handful fresh basil

¼ cup (25 g) finely shredded Parmigiano Reggiano

2 tablespoons (15 g) pistachios, lightly toasted and roughly chopped

My first taste of this pesto had me wondering why pistachios weren't already my go-to for pesto. Bright, fresh, and bursting with flavor, the pistachio pesto is a must-make on its own. Paired up with melty, creamy Robiola cheese and mortadella on a pizza though, it goes next-level. While many classic preparations of this pizza add the mortadella post-bake, I like to include it from the start. The heat of the oven crisps the slices slightly and renders some of the fat in magnificent ways.

1 **To make the Pistachio Pesto:** Combine the pistachios and garlic in the bowl of a small food processor. Pulse till finely chopped. Add the basil, lemon juice, and half of the olive oil and process until no whole basil leaves remain. Add the Parmigiano Reggiano and remaining olive oil and process till mostly smooth, adding more olive oil if the consistency is too thick. Season to taste with kosher salt and black pepper. Transfer to an airtight container and set aside until ready to top the pizza. The Pistachio Pesto can be stored in an airtight container in the refrigerator for up to 2 weeks.

2 **To make the pizza:** Preheat your indoor pizza oven with the temperature set to 850°F (454°C). When fully heated, set the heat balance dial (if equipped) to Bottom 0/Top 10.

3 Stretch your pizza dough to 10 to 12 inches (25 to 30 cm) (see stretching techniques p. 10). Leaving room for the crust to rise, spread about ¼ cup (65 g) of the Pistachio Pesto all over the pizza. Top the Pistachio Pesto with the Robiola cheese. Fold each slice of mortadella in half before draping across the pizza from the center toward the crust in a floral pattern.

4 Check the temperature of the baking stone. It should be around 800°F to 900°F (427°C to 482°C) when loading the pizza into

the oven. Slide the pizza onto the center of the baking stone and bake for 1 to 2 minutes, turning once or twice with a turning peel for an even bake. If the bottom of the pizza is baking too quickly, adjust the balance dial. If the bottom becomes too blackened but the top needs additional time, lift the pizza off the baking stone using a turning peel and hold it close to the roof of the oven to quickly finish cooking the top.

YIELD:
One 10-inch (25-cm) to 12-inch (30-cm) pizza

5 Look for the top and bottom of the crust to brown with lots of tiny dark spots all over and the mortadella to have crisped up slightly in some spots. The crust should feel set and not too floppy when picked up with a turning peel. When fully baked, remove the pizza from the oven and transfer to a wire rack to let the crust briefly set for about 30 seconds.

6 Transfer the pizza to a wooden peel to slice and slide the pizza onto a serving tray or plate. Tear the basil directly onto the pizza and top each slice with a dollop of Pistachio Pesto. Shower the pizza in Parmigiano Reggiano and pistachios. Serve immediately.

SPICY SOPPRESSATA PIZZA
WITH PICKLED SHALLOTS

FOR THE PICKLED SHALLOTS:

1 pound (455 g) shallots, sliced

1 clove garlic, peeled

1 teaspoon whole coriander seeds

1 teaspoon whole black peppercorns

1 bay leaf

1 cup (235 ml) water

1 cup (235 ml) red wine vinegar

¼ cup (60 ml) balsamic vinegar

1 tablespoon (14 g) kosher salt

2 teaspoons sugar

FOR THE PIZZA:

1 Neapolitan-Style Pizza Dough ball (see p. 79)

3 ounces (85 g) Neapolitan-Style Rustic Red Sauce (see p. 81)

¼ teaspoon dried oregano

1–2 Calabrian chiles in oil, chopped

4 ounces (115 g) fresh mozzarella cheese pearls

2 ounces (55 g) sliced spicy soppressata

Small handful fresh basil

¼ cup (20 g) finely shredded Pecorino Romano

W as spicy soppressata the original pepperoni? Probably not, but this pizza sure makes it feel like it. I love the kick of red chili with the slightly acidic bite of something pickled. Here, I go with shallots quick-pickled in red wine vinegar. Shallots, overall, are an underrated pizza topping. Their size and flavor are perfect for pizza. Pickled, they're addictive. You'll be putting these on anything needing a little bright blast of flavor.

1   **To make the Pickled Shallots** (24 hours before making pizza): Place the shallots in a quart-size (946 ml) deli container or mason jar. Place the garlic, coriander seeds, peppercorns, and bay leaf in the center of a piece of cheesecloth or parchment paper and fold into a package and secure with a silicone cooking band or kitchen twine. Combine the water, vinegars, kosher salt, and sugar in a heavy-duty saucepot. Add the package of aromatics and bring to a simmer to dissolve. Pour over the shallots to cover. A small piece of parchment paper can be placed over the liquid to keep the shallots submerged, if necessary. Let cool and transfer to the refrigerator for 24 hours. Remove the aromatics and discard. The Pickled Shallots can be stored in an airtight container in the refrigerator for up to 3 weeks.

2   **To make the pizza:** Ladle the sauce into the center of the pizza and spread it out towards the crust in a circular motion, leaving about 1 ½ inches (3.8 cm) of the outer crust bare. Sprinkle the sauce all over with the oregano and the chopped chiles. Scatter the mozzarella cheese pearls all over the pizza, leaving room for the sauce to still be visible after it melts. It should take about 15 small pieces of cheese. Top with the soppressata and 2 tablespoons drained Pickled Shallots.

3 Check the temperature of the baking stone. It should be around 800°F to 900°F (427°C to 482°C) when loading the pizza into the oven. Slide the pizza onto the center of the baking stone and bake for 1 to 2 minutes, turning once or twice with a turning peel for an even bake. If the bottom of the pizza is baking too quickly, adjust the balance dial. If the bottom becomes too blackened but the top needs additional time, lift the pizza off the baking stone using a turning peel and hold it close to the roof of the oven to quickly finish cooking the top.

4 Look for the top and bottom of the crust to brown with lots of tiny dark spots all over and the edges of the soppressata to have crisped a bit. The crust should feel set and not too floppy when picked up with a turning peel. When fully baked, remove the pizza from the oven and transfer to a wire rack to let the crust briefly set for about 30 seconds.

5 Transfer the pizza to a wooden peel to slice and slide the pizza onto a serving tray or plate. Tear the basil leaves on to the finished pizza and shower with Pecorino Romano. Serve immediately.

YIELD:
One 10-inch
(25-cm) to 12-inch
(30-cm) pizza

Chapter 5
Sicilian-Style Pan Pizzas

The Sicilian-style pizza commonly found in American pizzerias traces its origins to the tomato, onion, and anchovy–topped focaccia-style pizza found in Sicily, commonly known as *sfincione*. After reaching the United States, this style of pizza grew thicker and the shape became square. Topped with ingredients common in Italian-American kitchens, the Sicilian-style square pizza became a standard at pizzerias all over the east coast of the United States. It's typically sold by the slice alongside the thin-crusted, foldable, New York–style slices.

Sicilian-style squares are a favorite of mine to serve a crowd without stressing. The dough can be par-baked ahead of time, great for keeping things low-key for the final topping and baking.

EQUIPMENT AND TOOLS

10-INCH X 10-INCH (25-CM X 25-CM) SICILIAN-STYLE PIZZA PAN

Sicilian-style pizza pans are typically square, aluminum pans about 1½ inches (3.8 cm) deep. While pans designed specifically for pizza produce the best results with the greatest ease, a square cake pan will work for these recipes as well.

PAN GRABBER OR OVEN GLOVES

A metal pan grabber or a good set of oven gloves are crucial for easily and safely maneuvering the pans while in the oven as well as removing the hot pizzas from the pan. A pan grabber is especially handy for holding the pan steady while freeing the cheesy, crispy crust from the pan.

HEAVYWEIGHT METAL TURNER SPATULA

A heavyweight, metal turner spatula works well for removing Sicilian-style pizza from the pan. The heavy weight helps it free the edges and supports the pizza as you lift it out of the pan.

ROCKER-STYLE PIZZA CUTTER

The large, rocker-style pizza cutters are great for slicing Sicilian-style pizza. The thick blade and style make it easier to cut cleanly through the thicker crust versus wheel-style pizza cutters.

PIZZA SCREEN AND TRAY FOR SERVING

I like to serve this on a pizza screen nested in a pizza tray to keep it crisp while serving. A little bit of airflow under the warm pizza prevents a steamed, soggy bottom.

SICILIAN-STYLE BUTTER-CRUST PIZZA
DOUGH

170 grams filtered water, room temperature

8 grams kosher salt

2 grams instant dry yeast

230 grams bread flour

10 grams dark rye flour

10 grams softened unsalted butter

5 grams cold unsalted butter

¼ cup (60 ml) Sicilian-Style Pizza Sauce (see p. 96)

Avocado oil or olive oil, as needed

A Sicilian-style pizza dough is light, crispy, and buttery. For this style of pizza, I prefer to par-bake the dough before topping. The result is an exceptionally crisp crust with a soft interior. Butter is incorporated into the dough for a bit of added flavor and to increase the tenderness of this easy-to-make and easy-to-bake pizza dough.

1 Pour the filtered water into a large mixing bowl, add the salt, and stir to dissolve completely. Sprinkle the yeast on the surface of the water and let the yeast absorb some of the water for about 1 minute before stirring to dissolve completely. Add both flours.

2 Using your hands, mix the ingredients, stirring and pinching with your fingers till all the ingredients are fully incorporated and no dry flour remains. Cover and let rest at room temperature (about 70°F [21°C]) for 20 minutes.

3 After 20 minutes, uncover the dough, add the 10 grams of softened butter, and knead for 1 to 2 minutes directly in the bowl until the butter is fully incorporated. Cover and let rest at room temperature (about 70°F [21°C]) for 45 minutes to 1 hour.

4 After 45 minutes to an hour, uncover the dough and knead the dough for 1 minute. Cover the dough and let rest at room temperature (about 70°F [21°C]) for 30 minutes.

5 Grease the inside of a 10-inch x 10-inch (25 cm x 25 cm) Sicilian-style pizza pan with the remaining 5 grams of cold butter. ➤➤

YIELD:
1 pizza dough ball for one 10-inch (25-cm) x 10-inch (25-cm) pizza

6 Uncover the dough and shape into a ball using your hands, folding the dough into itself a couple times. Place the dough ball in the center of the pan and cover. Let the dough relax in the pan for about 10 minutes.

7 Press the dough ball down into the pan. Pour a small amount of avocado or olive oil on your hands and use your fingers to work the dough toward the edges of the pan, pushing it out and resisting the urge to pick the dough up from the pan too much as you may trap air underneath. If the dough is difficult to work, cover and let rest for about 5 minutes before working the dough again. Repeat the process. It takes about 2 to 3 rest cycles to fully stretch the dough.

8 Once fully stretched, cover the pan and transfer to the refrigerator to cold ferment for at least 12 hours and up to 72 hours.

9 **6 to 8 hours before par-baking:** Remove the pan from the refrigerator and let the dough rise, covered, at room temperature (about 70°F [21°C]) for 6 to 8 hours before baking. Look for the dough to have expanded and risen with lots of small bubbles on the surface.

10 **To par-bake the dough:** Preheat your indoor pizza oven with the temperature set to 450°F (230°C). When the pizza oven is fully heated, set the heat balance dial (if equipped) to Bottom 5/Top 5.

11 Brush the crust with a thin layer of Sicilian-Style Pizza Sauce, about ¼ cup (60 ml).

12 Check the temperature of the baking stone. It should be around 450°F to 500°F (230°C to 250°C) when loading the pizza into the oven. Slide the pan onto the center of the baking stone and bake for 10 to 12 minutes, turning a few times as it bakes.

13 When properly par-baked, the sides of the crust should pull away from the edges of the pan and the top of the crust should be light golden brown in color. Use caution to not overbake.

14 Remove the pan from the oven and let rest for about 30 seconds. Using a metal spatula, carefully remove the par-baked crust and invert (bottom of the crust facing up) on to a wire rack to cool. Let cool completely on the rack, inverted, before making the pizza. Alternatively, the par-baked crust can be wrapped in plastic and stored in the refrigerator for up to 4 days or in the freezer for a few months. Bring to room temperature before using.

SICILIAN-STYLE PIZZA
SAUCE

1 can (28 ounces, or 785 ml) crushed tomatoes

1 small onion, peeled and cut in half

2 tablespoons (32 g) tomato paste

1 clove garlic, minced

1 teaspoon dried oregano

½ teaspoon dried basil

¼ teaspoon garlic powder

1 teaspoon kosher salt

My Sicilian-style pizza sauce is "lightly touched" with a brief simmer with aromatics for a flavor that's fresh yet full. The halved onion is simmered in the sauce for flavor but removed before the rest of the sauce is pureed for a rich taste and smooth texture.

1 Combine the tomatoes, onion, tomato paste, garlic, oregano, basil, garlic powder, and salt in a saucepan. Bring to a simmer over medium heat. Simmer, stirring often, till the flavors have combined and the sauce has reduced slightly, 15 to 20 minutes. Remove the onion and discard.

2 Using an immersion blender, puree the sauce till mostly smooth. Season to taste with salt. Let cool before topping pizza. The Sicilian-Style Pizza Sauce can be stored in an airtight container in the refrigerator for up to a week.

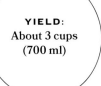

YIELD:
About 3 cups
(700 ml)

CLASSIC SICILIAN
SQUARE

1 tablespoon (14 g) unsalted butter

1 par-baked Sicilian-Style Butter-Crust Pizza Dough (see p. 93)

3 ounces (85 g) low-moisture whole-milk mozzarella cheese, thickly shredded

3 ounces (85 g) fontina cheese, thickly shredded

¾ cup (175 ml) Sicilian-Style Pizza Sauce (see p. 96)

¼ teaspoon dried oregano

Small handful fresh basil

¼ cup (25 g) finely shredded Parmigiano Reggiano

2 tablespoons (28 ml) extra-virgin olive oil

simple square pillow of dough slathered in sauce, topped with cheese, and even more sauce is something super satisfying. The par-baked, buttery Sicilian-Style Butter-Crust Pizza Dough stays crisp and light, topped "upside-down" for my tribute to a traditional Sicilian-style square.

1 Preheat your indoor pizza oven with the temperature set to 450°F (230°C). When the pizza oven is fully heated, set the heat balance dial (if equipped) to Bottom 5/Top 5.

2 Grease the inside of a 10-inch x 10-inch (25-cm x 25-cm) Sicilian-style pizza pan with butter. Transfer the par-baked dough to the pan. Combine the mozzarella cheese and fontina cheese in a bowl. Scatter the shredded cheese mixture all over the top of the pizza. Apply the sauce in 5 to 7 diagonal lines across the top of the pizza, 1 to 2 inches (2.5 to 5 cm) wide. Sprinkle with oregano.

3 Check the temperature of the baking stone. It should be around 450°F to 500°F (230°C to 250°C) when loading the pizza into the oven. Slide the pan onto the center of the baking stone and bake for 10 to 12 minutes, turning a few times as it bakes. ➤➤

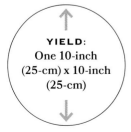

YIELD:
One 10-inch
(25-cm) x 10-inch
(25-cm)

4 When fully baked, the cheese should be melted and the crust golden brown in color. Remove the pan from the oven and let rest for about 30 seconds. Using a metal spatula, carefully remove the pizza from the pan and transfer to a metal rack to cool for about 1 minute.

5 Transfer the pizza to a wooden peel to slice and slide the pizza onto your serving tray or plate. Tear the basil leaves onto the finished pizza, shower with Parmigiano Reggiano, and drizzle with extra-virgin olive oil. Serve immediately.

SUPREME SUNDAY
SQUARE

FOR THE SAUSAGE AND PANCETTA TOPPING:

4 ounces (115 g) diced pancetta

6 ounces (170 g) sweet Italian sausage (or home-made Fennel Sausage see p. 67), casing removed

FOR THE CARAMELIZED ONIONS:

1 small yellow onion, sliced

Kosher salt to taste

FOR THE ROASTED PEPPERS:

1 red bell pepper

1 jalapeño pepper (optional)

FOR THE PIZZA:

1 tablespoon (14 g) unsalted butter

1 par-baked Sicilian-Style Butter-Crust Pizza Dough (see p. 93)

3 ounces (85 g) low-moisture whole-milk mozzarella cheese, thickly shredded

3 ounces (85 g) fontina cheese, thickly shredded

¼ teaspoon dried oregano

Small handful fresh basil

1 clove garlic, minced

The Sunday square became a tradition at our house thanks to the OG pizza blogger, Adam Kuban. It's a big, square pizza that's easy to make and satisfies the whole family. You spend less time fussing with some flour and more time with the fam. Load it with hearty toppings that are easy to prepare ahead of time to make it especially low fuss.

1   **To make the Sausage and Pancetta Topping:** Heat a large skillet over medium-high heat and add the diced pancetta. Let the pancetta cook briefly, rendering some of the fat, and add the sausage. Break up any large pieces of sausage and continue cooking until just browned. Use a slotted spoon to remove the cooked sausage and pancetta, reserving any rendered fat in the pan to cook the Caramelized Onions. Let cool in a small bowl. The Sausage and Pancetta Topping can be stored in an airtight container in the refrigerator for 3 to 4 days.

2   **To make the Caramelized Onions:** Heat the rendered sausage and pancetta fat over medium heat and add the sliced onion. After the onion has released some moisture, turn the heat to low and continue cooking until the onions are lightly caramelized, 20 to 30 minutes. Remove from heat and season to taste with salt. Let cool before topping pizza. The Caramelized Onions can be stored in an airtight container in the refrigerator for up to 4 days.

3   **To make the Roasted Peppers:** Using an oven broiler or gas-powered cooktop, blacken the outside of the peppers till completely charred and the skin begins to flake away. Place in a bowl and cover tightly with plastic wrap. Let rest until cool enough to handle. Peel away the charred skin and dispose of the core and seeds. Dice the roasted peppers and set aside till ready to top the pizza. The Roasted Peppers can be stored in an airtight container in the refrigerator for 4 to 5 days.

½ cup (120 ml) Sicilian-Style Pizza Sauce (see p. 96)

3 ounces (85 g) sliced pepperoni

¼ cup (25 g) finely shredded Parmigiano Reggiano

4 **To make the pizza:** Preheat your indoor pizza oven with the temperature set to 450°F (230°C). When the pizza oven is fully heated, set the heat balance dial (if equipped) to Bottom 5/Top 5.

5 Grease the inside of a 10-inch x 10-inch (25-cm x 25-cm) Sicilian-style pizza pan with butter. Transfer the par-baked dough to the pan. Combine the mozzarella cheese and fontina cheese in a bowl.

6 Scatter the shredded cheese mixture all over the top of the pizza. Sprinkle with oregano. Tear half the basil leaves onto the pizza. Top with the Sausage and Pancetta Topping, followed by the Caramelized Onions, garlic, and Roasted Peppers. Apply the sauce in diagonal lines across the top of the pizza, about 1-inch (2.5 cm) wide. Top with the pepperoni.

7 Check the temperature of the baking stone. It should be around 450°F to 500°F (230°C to 250°C) when loading the pizza into the oven. Slide the pan onto the center of the baking stone and bake for 10 to 12 minutes, turning a few times as it bakes.

8 When fully baked, the cheese should be melted and the pepperoni should be cupped and crisped up in spots. Remove the pan from the oven and let rest for about 30 seconds. Using a metal spatula, carefully remove the pizza from the pan and transfer to a metal rack to cool for about 1 minute.

9 Transfer the pizza to a wooden peel to slice and slide the pizza onto a serving tray or plate. Tear the remaining basil leaves on to the finished pizza and shower with Parmigiano Reggiano. Serve immediately.

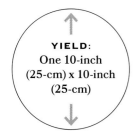

YIELD:
One 10-inch (25-cm) x 10-inch (25-cm)

GARDEN HARVEST
SICILIAN

FOR THE CURED AND ROASTED SUMMER SQUASH:

1 small green zucchini, sliced into thin coins

1 small yellow summer squash, sliced into thin coins

1 teaspoon kosher salt

1 tablespoon (15 ml) extra-virgin olive oil

¼ teaspoon dried oregano

¼ teaspoon fresh thyme

FOR THE MARINATED TOMATOES:

1 large tomato, diced

1 small shallot, minced

1 clove garlic, minced

1 tablespoon (15 ml) olive oil

1 teaspoon red wine vinegar

2–3 basil leaves, chopped

¼ teaspoon dried oregano

Kosher salt to taste

Freshly ground black pepper to taste

FOR THE PIZZA:

1 tablespoon (14 g) unsalted butter

1 par-baked Sicilian-Style Butter-Crust Pizza Dough (see p. 93)

T his is the summer's harvest on a Sicilian square. When the bounty of your garden is overflowing, make this pizza. The trick to coaxing out the most intense flavors of your summer squash is a quick cure and low-temperature roast to pull out the overflowing moisture within. On the square, they join my favorite summer harvest item, garden-fresh tomatoes. When it's their season, don't forget to seize the moment and put them on a pizza.

1 **To make the Cured and Roasted Summer Squash:** Combine the zucchini, yellow summer squash, and salt in a bowl and toss well to combine. Transfer the mixture to a colander positioned over a bowl or sink and let drain, tossing occasionally, about 1 hour. Preheat a home oven to 250°F (120°C, or gas mark ½). Dry the squash mixture of excess moisture on a clean kitchen towel and transfer to a bowl. Add the olive oil, oregano, and thyme and toss well. Transfer to a sheet pan lined with foil and lightly roast until soft and cooked through, but not darkened, 30 to 45 minutes. Let cool before topping pizza. The Cured and Roasted Summer Squash can be stored in an airtight container in the refrigerator for 2 to 3 days.

2 **To make the Marinated Tomatoes:** Combine the diced tomato, shallot, garlic, olive oil, vinegar, basil, and oregano in a bowl. Season to taste with kosher salt and black pepper. Set aside until ready to top the pizza. The Marinated Tomatoes can be stored in an airtight container in the refrigerator for 2 to 3 days.

3 **To make the pizza:** Preheat your indoor pizza oven with the temperature set to 450°F (230°C). When the pizza oven is fully heated, set the heat balance dial (if equipped) to Bottom 5/Top 5.

4 ounces (115 g) low-moisture whole-milk mozzarella cheese, thickly shredded

2 ounces (55 g) feta cheese

1 roasted red pepper, diced (see technique on p. 100)

2 tablespoons (28 ml) Pickled Shallots, drained (see p. 88)

Small handful fresh basil

1 tablespoon (15 ml) balsamic vinegar

YIELD:
One 10-inch (25-cm) x 10-inch (25-cm)

4 Grease the inside of a 10-inch x 10-inch (25-cm x 25-cm) Sicilian-style pizza pan with butter. Transfer the par-baked dough to the pan. Scatter the mozzarella cheese all over the top of the pizza. Top with 1 cup (180 g) Cured and Roasted Summer Squash. Crumble the feta cheese evenly over the squash. Top with the Marinated Tomatoes (drained of excess liquid), roasted pepper, and Pickled Shallots.

5 Check the temperature of the baking stone. It should be around 450°F to 500°F (230°C to 250°C) when loading the pizza into the oven. Slide the pan onto the center of the baking stone and bake for 10 to 12 minutes, turning a few times as it bakes.

6 When fully baked, the cheese should be melted. Remove the pan from the oven and let rest for about 30 seconds. Using a metal spatula, carefully remove the pizza from the pan and transfer to a metal rack to cool for about 1 minute.

7 Transfer the pizza to a wooden peel to slice and slide the pizza onto your serving tray or plate. Tear the basil leaves on to the finished pizza and drizzle with balsamic vinegar. Serve immediately.

EPIC GARLIC
CHEESY BREAD

FOR THE ROASTED GARLIC:
1 large head of garlic

FOR THE GARLIC BUTTER:
¼ cup (55 g) unsalted butter

1 tablespoon (15 ml) extra-virgin olive oil

2 cloves garlic, minced

¼ teaspoon garlic powder

¼ teaspoon dried oregano

Pinch red pepper flakes

FOR THE PIZZA:
1 dough ball Sicilian-Style Butter-Crust Pizza Dough, panned for final proofing (see p. 93)

5 ounces (140 g) whole-milk mozzarella cheese, thickly shredded

1 clove garlic, minced

¼ teaspoon dried oregano

½ cup (50 g) finely shredded Parmigiano Reggiano, divided

The ultimate in epic, garlicky, cheesy, and buttery bread. The crust gets stuffed with whole cloves of sweet, roasted garlic and then bathed in garlic butter, blanketed in cheese, and showered with even more garlic. That may sound over the top, but trust me, it's just right.

1 **To make the Roasted Garlic:** Preheat a home oven to 350°F (180°C, or gas mark 4). Trim the bottom of the head of garlic with a knife, removing the roots and thick outer skin, but keeping the cloves whole. Wrap the head of garlic in aluminum foil and roast until completely tender, 45 minutes to 1 hour. Let cool. Unwrap the head of garlic and separate the cloves, peeling away and discarding any skins or papery bits. Set aside until ready to make the pizza. The roasted garlic can be stored in an airtight container in the refrigerator for up to 3 days.

2 **To make the Garlic Butter:** Melt the butter in a small saucepan over medium-low heat. Add the olive oil, garlic, garlic powder, oregano, and red pepper flakes. Reduce the heat to low and cook, stirring often, until the garlic has softened and is very fragrant, about 5 minutes. Don't let it brown. Let cool to room temperature before topping pizza. The Garlic Butter can be stored in an airtight container in the refrigerator for up to 5 days.

3 **To make the pizza (6 to 8 hours before baking):** Remove the pan from the refrigerator. Push the whole cloves of Roasted Garlic into the dough about ½-inch (0.6 cm) apart and let the dough rise, covered, at room temperature (about 70°F [21°C]) for 1 to 2 hours. Uncover the dough and push the Roasted Garlic cloves back into the dough if they have become dislodged as the dough rose. Cover and continue proofing at room temperature for 4 to 6 hours. Look for the dough to have expanded and risen with lots of small bubbles on the surface.

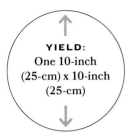

4 When ready to bake the pizza, preheat your indoor pizza oven with the temperature set to 450°F (230°C). When the pizza oven is fully heated, set the heat balance dial (if equipped) to Bottom 5/Top 5.

5 Uncover the proofed dough and brush the surface of the dough generously with ¼ cup (60 ml) Garlic Butter, melted and cooled but still liquid. Scatter the cheese all over the top of the pizza. Sprinkle with the minced garlic and oregano. Top with half of the Parmigiano Reggiano.

6 Check the temperature of the baking stone. It should be around 450°F to 500°F (230°C to 250°C) when loading the pizza into the oven. Slide the pan onto the center of the baking stone and bake for 15 to 18 minutes, turning a few times as it bakes.

7 When fully baked, the crust should have pulled away from the sides of the pan and browned. The cheese should be fully melted and browned in some spots. Remove the pan from the oven and let rest for about 30 seconds. Using a metal spatula, carefully remove the pizza from the pan and transfer to a metal rack to cool for about 1 minute.

8 Transfer the pizza to a wooden peel to slice and slide the pizza onto your serving tray or plate. Shower with the remaining Parmigiano Reggiano and serve immediately.

SICILIAN-STYLE PAN PIZZAS

Chapter 6
Detroit-Style Pan Pizzas

Thick-crust pizza often looks heavy, but this Detroit-style pizza is light as a feather. Once mostly a Motor City specialty, this style has spread worldwide in recent years. It's no surprise. It's super satisfying and straightforward to make at home. During its travels, Detroit-style pizza has morphed and evolved way beyond its original preparation. Here, I try to stay close to its origins when possible.

Indoor pizza ovens equipped with the ability to balance the heat between the bottom and the top of the oven are especially good at making authentic Detroit-style pizza. Directing the heat to the bottom of the pizza prevents the cheese and toppings from burning as the base bakes into a beautiful brown crispness.

EQUIPMENT AND TOOLS

8-INCH X 10-INCH (20-CM X 25-CM) DETROIT-STYLE PIZZA PAN

Traditionally, Detroit-style pizza was baked in rectangular blue steel pans that were commonly used to hold small automotive parts as part of the bustling Detroit auto industry. Nowadays, these pans are specifically made for pizza and feature high, sloped sides that are about 2 ½ inches (6.3 cm) deep with a coating that makes the pizzas easy to release. The 8-inch x 10-inch (20-cm x 25-cm) size is a traditional size for Detroit-style pizza and fits in the largest variety of indoor pizza ovens.

PAN GRABBER OR OVEN GLOVES

A metal pan grabber or a good set of oven gloves are crucial for easily and safely maneuvering the pans while in the oven as well as removing the hot pizzas from the pan. A pan grabber is especially handy for holding the pan steady while freeing the cheesy, crispy crust from the pan.

HEAVYWEIGHT METAL TURNER SPATULA

A heavyweight metal turner spatula excels at easily removing Detroit-style pizza from the pan. The heavy weight helps it slide down the edge of the pan, freeing the cheese crown and supporting the pizza as you lift it out of the deepness.

ROCKER-STYLE PIZZA CUTTER

The large, rocker-style pizza cutters are perfect for cutting Detroit-style pizza. The thick blade and style make it easier to cut cleanly through the deep-dish crust versus wheel-style pizza cutters.

QUARTER SHEET PAN WITH WIRE RACK

I serve my Detroit-style pizzas on a wire rack nested inside a quarter sheet pan. The rack helps keep the bottom of the pizza crisp.

DETROIT-STYLE PIZZA
DOUGH

110 grams filtered water

5 grams kosher salt

1 gram instant dry yeast

155 grams bread flour (Recommended: King Arthur Bread Flour or Central Milling Central Milling "High Mountain" Flour

1–2 teaspoons unsalted butter

YIELD:
1 pizza dough ball for one 8-inch (20-cm) x 10-inch (25-cm) pizza

Featherlight but delightfully crisp and sturdy, it's a dreamy cloud of dough capable of holding stacks of toppings.

1 Pour the filtered water into a large mixing bowl, add the salt, and stir to dissolve completely. Sprinkle the yeast on the surface of the water and let the yeast absorb some of the water for about 1 minute before stirring to dissolve completely. Add the flour.

2 Using your hands, mix the ingredients, stirring and pinching with your fingers till all the ingredients are fully incorporated and no dry flour remains. The high hydration of this dough can make it feel sticky. A light splash of water on your hands can help prevent the dough from clinging to your hands. Cover and let rest at room temperature (about 70°F [21°C]) for 20 to 30 minutes. This rest gives the flour some time to absorb the water and makes the dough easier to knead.

3 After 20 to 30 minutes, uncover the dough and knead for 1 to 2 minutes directly in the bowl till mostly smooth, but before it becomes too sticky too handle. Cover and let rest at room temperature (about 70°F [21°C]) for 45 minutes to 1 hour.

4 After the rest, uncover the dough and knead briefly in the bowl or in your hands. Cover the dough and let rest for about 10 minutes while you prepare the Detroit-style pizza pan.

5 Using your hands, rub the butter all over the inside of an 8-inch (20-cm) x 10-inch (25-cm) Detroit-style pizza pan. You want a thin layer covering the surface, taking care to make sure the corners of the pan are well greased. ➤➤

1 Detroit-style pizza dough ready to be stretched and panned in a greased 8-inch (20-cm) x 10-inch (25-cm) Detroit-style pizza pan.

2 Detroit-style pizza dough stretched to the edges of the pan after three stretch and rest cycles. The dough is now ready for the final rise and fermentation.

3 Fully proofed Detroit-style pizza dough ready to baked. The dough has risen up the sides of the pan and around the chunks of pepperoni.

4 Par-baked Detroit-style pizza ready to be topped and baked.

6 Uncover the dough and shape into a ball using your hands, folding the dough into itself a couple times. It's helpful to do this while you still have butter on your hands from greasing the pan. Place the dough ball in the center of the pan and cover. Let the dough relax in the pan for about 10 minutes.

7 Press the dough ball down into the pan. Using your fingers, work the dough towards the edges of the pan, pushing it out and resisting the urge to pick the dough up from the pan too much as you may trap air underneath. If the dough is difficult to work, cover and let rest for about 5 minutes before working the dough again. Repeat the process. It takes about 2 to 3 rest cycles to fully stretch the dough.

8 Once fully stretched, cover the pan and transfer to the refrigerator to cold ferment for at least 12 hours and up to 72 hours.

9 **6 to 8 hours before making the Classic Detroit-Style Pizza or par-baking for other recipes:** Remove the pan from the refrigerator and let the dough rise, covered, at room temperature (about 70°F [21°C]) for 6 to 8 hours before baking. Look for the dough to have expanded and risen with lots of small bubbles on the surface.

10 **To par-bake the dough:** Preheat your indoor pizza oven with the temperature set to 500°F (260°C). When the pizza oven is fully heated, set the heat balance dial (if equipped) to Bottom 5/ Top 5. ➤➤

11 Check the temperature of the baking stone. It should be around 500°F to 550°F (260°C to 288°C) when loading the pizza into the oven. Slide the pan onto the center of the baking stone and bake for 10 to 12 minutes, turning a few times as it bakes. When properly par-baked, the sides of the crust should pull away from the edges of the pan and the top of the crust should be light golden brown in color. Use caution to not overbake.

12 Remove the pan from the oven and let rest for about 30 seconds. Using a metal spatula, carefully remove the par-baked crust and invert (bottom of the crust facing up) on to a wire rack to cool. Let cool completely on the rack, inverted, before making the pizza. Alternatively, the par-baked crust can be wrapped in plastic and stored in the refrigerator for up to 4 days or in the freezer for a few months. Bring to room temperature before using.

DETROIT-STYLE PIZZA
SAUCE

1 can (28 ounces, or
785 ml) crushed tomatoes
or tomato puree

1 tube (4.5 ounces, or 128 g)
tomato paste

½ teaspoon dried oregano

Kosher salt to taste

Detroit-style pizza sauce is a simple affair. Texture is key; you don't want it to be watery or it will run off the top of the crust and down the sides, resulting in a soggy crust. To combat any sogginess, I reach for crushed tomatoes or tomato puree. They tend to be thicker and loaded with intense tomato flavor.

1 Combine the tomatoes, tomato paste, and oregano in a large pot or blender. Blend with an immersion blender or blend on high until completely smooth.

2 Season to taste with kosher salt. The Detroit-Style Pizza Sauce can be stored in an airtight container in the refrigerator for up to a week.

YIELD:
About 1 quart
(946 ml)

CLASSIC DETROIT-STYLE
PIZZA

¼ teaspoon dried oregano

1 Detroit-Style Pizza Dough ball, panned, proofed, and ready for baking (see p. 109)

12 slices pepperoni

3 ounces (85 g) Munster cheese, cubed

3 ounces (85 g) low-moisture whole-milk mozzarella cheese, cubed

3½ ounces (99 g) Detroit-Style Pizza Sauce (see p. 113)

Staying true to the classic preparation at Detroit pizzerias such as Buddy's Pizza, this is the Motor City's finest, made at home. The classic preparation doesn't include par-baking the dough. Instead, the unbaked dough is topped "upside-down" with the pepperoni below the cheese and sauce. Wisconsin "brick cheese" along with low-moisture mozzarella cheese is traditional, but I've found the brick cheese to be difficult to find locally and expensive to order online. As a substitute, I head to the deli counter for a thick slab of Munster cheese. It's the best I've found for recreating that distinct, rich, and buttery flavor without having to travel all the way to Detroit.

1 Preheat your indoor pizza oven with the temperature set to 450°F (230°C). When the pizza oven is fully heated, set the heat balance dial (if equipped) to Bottom 9/Top 1.

2 Sprinkle the oregano over the top of the pizza dough. Gently lay the sliced pepperoni in 3 rows of 4 lengthwise over the top of the pizza. Scatter the cubed cheeses all over the top of the pizza, making sure plenty ends up along the edges of the pan. This will create the signature crispy cheese "frico" crust. Use a spoon to dot the top of the pizza with the sauce in 2 straight lines.

3 Load the pizza into the pizza oven, placing the pan in the center of the baking stone. Bake for 15 to 18 minutes, rotating the pan about halfway through the bake. As the pizza bakes, the crust will pull away from the sides of the pan and crisp. Carefully check the crust as the pizza finishes baking, looking for a golden-brown crust that has mostly freed itself from the edges of the pan and fully melted but not burned cheese.

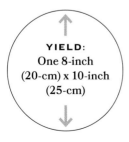

YIELD:
One 8-inch
(20-cm) x 10-inch
(25-cm)

4 Remove the pan from the oven and let cool for about 1 minute. Taking care to preserve the frico crust, insert a metal spatula along the edge of the pan and fully free the pizza before removing. Transfer the pizza to a wire rack to let the crust set for about 1 minute before slicing on a cutting board.

5 Transfer the sliced pizza to a wire rack nested in a quarter sheet pan to stay crisp while serving. Serve immediately.

THE EPIC PEPPERONI-STUFFED-AND-CRUSTED
PIZZA

1 Detroit-Style Pizza Dough, panned and prepared for the final rise (see p. 109)

1½ ounces (43 g) pepperoni, diced into small pieces from a whole stick

1 tablespoon (14 g) butter

30 slices pepperoni

¼ teaspoon dried oregano

3 ounces (85 g) shredded pizza cheese blend or mozzarella

5 ounces (140 g) low-moisture whole-milk mozzarella cheese, cubed

4 ounces (120 ml) Detroit-Style Pizza Sauce (see p. 113)

5 ounces (140 g) cupping pepperoni

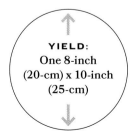

YIELD:
One 8-inch
(20-cm) x 10-inch
(25-cm)

Stuffed and stacked with pepperoni, this is the ultimate in pepperoni pizza. There's guaranteed pepperoni in every bite, thanks to a pepperoni-enrobed crust stuffed with nuggets of pepperoni. To top it off, the pepperoni crust is layered with classic pepperoni and then showered with a generous amount of cupping pepperoni. Despite being made of an absolutely ridiculous amount of pepperoni, this pizza somehow manages to still be "light." I'm not sure how that's even possible, but I'm game.

A stuffed crust and an absolutely insane amount of pepperoni make par-baking the crust before topping the pizza way to go for this Detroit-style pizza.

1 **To make the pepperoni stuffed crust** (at least 8 hours before baking the pizza or the day before): Remove the panned dough from the refrigerator and uncover. Scatter the diced pepperoni all over the top of the pizza and gently push into the dough. Cover and let rise at room temperature (about 70°F [21°C]) for 1 to 2 hours. After 1 to 2 hours, the dough should have risen slightly. Gently push the diced pepperoni deeper into the rising dough so it becomes part of the crust. Cover and let proof for 4 to 6 hours at room temperature (about 70°F [21°C]).

2 Preheat your indoor pizza oven with the temperature set to 450°F (230°C). When the pizza oven is fully heated, set the heat balance dial (if equipped) to Bottom 5/Top 5.

3 Uncover the pan and load it into the oven, placing the pan in the center of the baking stone. Bake 10 to 12 minutes. The crust should be lightly golden brown on the bottom with a few golden-brown spots on the surface as well. ➤➤

4 Remove the pan from the oven and let rest for about 30 seconds. Using a metal spatula, carefully remove the par-baked crust and invert (bottom of the crust facing up) on to a wire rack to cool. Let cool completely on the rack, inverted, before making the pizza. Alternatively, the par-baked crust can be wrapped in plastic and stored in the refrigerator for up to 4 days or in the freezer for a few months. Bring to room temperature before using.

5 **To make the pizza:** Preheat your indoor pizza oven with the temperature set to 450°F (230°C). When the pizza oven is fully heated, set the heat balance dial (if equipped) to Bottom 5/Top 5.

6 Grease an 8-inch x 10-inch (20 cm x 25 cm) Detroit-style pizza pan with butter. Transfer the par-baked dough to the pan. Slide slices of pepperoni between the edge of the crust and the pan, slightly overlapping. It should take about 18 slices to line the entire crust. Sprinkle the entire pizza with the oregano and top the pizza with 12 slices of pepperoni in 3 rows of 4 lengthwise over the top of the crust. Tightly line the outer pepperoni crust with the shredded cheese. Scatter the cubed cheese all over the top of the pizza. Use a ladle to apply the sauce in 3 stripes lengthwise. Push the back of the ladle into the pizza gently to help spread the sauce out a bit but maintain the stripes. Cover the entire pizza in the cupping pepperoni. They will shrink significantly as it bakes, so don't be shy—go big.

7 Load the pan into the pizza oven, placing the pan in the center of the baking stone and bake for 12 to 15 minutes, rotating once or twice throughout the bake. Make sure the cheese is fully melted and the pepperoni cupped before removing it from the oven. Let the pan cool for about 1 minute before carefully removing the pizza using a metal spatula. Transfer the pizza to a wire rack to let the crust set for about 1 minute before slicing on a cutting board.

8 Transfer the sliced pizza to a wire rack nested in a quarter sheet pan to stay crisp while serving. Get ready to experience the most pepperoni-filled pepperoni pizza ever and dig in.

SPINACH AND ARTICHOKE PIZZA

FOR THE SPINACH AND ARTICHOKE TOPPING:

- 2 tablespoons (28 ml) extra-virgin olive oil
- 1 shallot, diced
- 2 cloves garlic, diced
- 1 jalapeño pepper, diced
- 8 ounces (225 g) frozen artichoke hearts (no need to thaw)
- 8 ounces (225 g) frozen chopped spinach (no need to thaw)
- 3 ounces (85 g) whole-milk ricotta cheese
- 3 ounces (85 g) fontina cheese, thickly shredded
- 1 lemon, juice and zest
- 1 cup (24 g) fresh basil leaves
- ¼ teaspoon garlic powder
- ¼ teaspoon onion powder
- Kosher salt to taste
- Freshly ground black pepper to taste

FOR THE PARMESAN BREADCRUMBS:

- ½ cup (56 g) panko breadcrumbs
- 2 ounces (55 g) Parmesan cheese, finely shredded

➸

Take the spinach and artichoke dip that you just can't stop eating, cross it with a crispy, crunchy Detroit-style pizza, and you get this. It's something special, and I highly recommend making it. You'll be fighting over the last slice.

1. **To make the Spinach and Artichoke Topping:** Heat the olive oil in large sauté pan over medium heat. Add the shallots, garlic, and jalapeño to the pan and cook till just soft, about 1 minute. Add the artichoke hearts to the pan and cook, stirring and breaking them as they soften, for 10 minutes. Add the spinach, 1 handful at a time, and cook till soft and wilted. Remove from the heat and let cool. Add the ricotta, fontina, lemon juice and zest, basil, garlic, and onion and mix well using a spoon. Season to taste with kosher salt and black pepper. Set aside till ready to top the pizza. The Spinach and Artichoke Topping can be stored in an airtight container in the refrigerator for 4 to 5 days.

2. **To make the Parmesan Breadcrumbs:** Combine the panko breadcrumbs and Parmesan cheese in a small bowl. Set aside till ready to top the pizza. The Parmesan Breadcrumbs can be stored in an airtight container in the refrigerator for 4 to 5 days.

3. **To make the pizza:** If the par-baked dough has been stored refrigerated, transfer from the refrigerator to the kitchen counter and let to come to room temperature.

4. Preheat your indoor pizza oven with the temperature set to 450°F (230°C). When the pizza oven is fully heated, set the heat balance dial (if equipped) to Bottom 5/Top 5. ➸

EPIC INDOOR PIZZA OVEN COOKBOOK

FOR THE PIZZA:
1 Detroit-Style Pizza Dough, par-baked (see p. 111)

1 tablespoon (14 g) butter

3 ounces (85 g) shredded pizza cheese blend

Small handful fresh basil

¼ cup (25 g) finely shredded Parmigiano Reggiano

5   Grease an 8-inch x 10-inch (20-cm x 25-cm) Detroit-style pizza pan with butter. Transfer the par-baked dough to the pan. Spread the shredded pizza cheese blend along the edges of the dough and between the crust and the side of the pan. This will create the frico cheese crown. Top with the Spinach and Artichoke Topping.

6   Load the pizza into the pizza oven, placing the pan in the center of the baking stone and bake for 12 to 15 minutes, rotating once or twice throughout the bake. When fully baked, the cheese should be melted and browned in some spots and the cheese crust should have pulled away from the sides of the pan. Once baked, remove the pan from the oven and let the pan cool for about 1 minute before carefully removing the pizza using a metal spatula. Transfer the pizza to a wire rack to let the crust set for about 1 minute before slicing on a cutting board.

7   Transfer the sliced pizza to a wire rack nested in a quarter sheet pan to stay crisp while serving. Tear the basil leaves on to the pizza and shower with the Parmigiano Reggiano. Serve immediately.

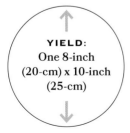

YIELD:
One 8-inch
(20-cm) x 10-inch
(25-cm)

GRILLED CHEESE PIZZA
WITH TOMATO SOUP DIP

FOR THE TOMATO SOUP:

2 tablespoons (28 g) unsalted butter

1 shallot, sliced

1 clove garlic, sliced

1 can (28 ounces, or 785 ml) whole peeled tomatoes

1 cup (235 ml) water or chicken stock

1 slice country loaf or white bread

½ teaspoon dried basil

2 tablespoons (28 ml) heavy cream

Kosher salt to taste

Freshly ground black pepper to taste

FOR THE TOP CRUST:

60 grams filtered water

3 grams kosher salt

0.5 grams instant dry yeast

FOR THE PIZZA:

3 tablespoons (42 g) unsalted butter, divided

1 clove garlic, peeled

¼ teaspoon garlic powder

3 ounces (85 g) low-moisture whole-milk mozzarella cheese, thickly shredded

1 ounce (28 g) Parmesan cheese, finely shredded

➤➤

B efore pizza, I made grilled cheese. Sometimes, hundreds a night, feeding the hungry fans of the band Phish. Grilled cheese is near and dear to my heart, so it gave me pause to transform it into a pizza. Then, I made one Detroit-style—wow, mind blown. It totally works. Crispy, cheesy, and buttery, this pizza is everything you want in a grilled cheese and a pizza. The slices are perfect for dipping and dunking into my simple and satisfying tomato soup. It's pure comfort. The top layer of dough takes a bit of lead time, so don't forget to get that started 6 to 8 hours before making the pizza.

1   **To make the Tomato Soup:** Melt the butter in large saucepan over medium heat. Add the shallot and garlic. Cook, stirring often, till the shallot and garlic are soft but not browned. Add the tomatoes and water or stock. Break the tomatoes up in the pan using a potato masher. Add the bread and basil. Bring to a boil over high and then reduce to a simmer. Cook for 15 minutes. Add the heavy cream and stir to combine. Transfer the soup to a blender. Alternatively, the soup may be blended directly in the pan using an immersion blender, but the texture won't be as smooth. Blend on the lowest speed and then gradually increase the speed to high. Blend till completely smooth. Season to taste with kosher salt and black pepper. Transfer the soup to a saucepan and keep warm till ready to serve. The tomato soup can be stored in an airtight container in the refrigerator for up to a week.

2   **To make the Top Crust** (6 to 8 hours before making the pizza): Pour the filtered water into a small mixing bowl, add the salt, and stir to dissolve completely. Sprinkle the yeast on the surface of the water and let the yeast absorb some of the water for about 1 minute before stirring to dissolve completely. Add the flour. Using your hands, mix the ingredients, stirring and pinching with your fingers till all the ingredients are fully incorporated and no ➤➤

1 Detroit-Style Pizza Dough, par-baked (see p. 111)

4 slices white cheddar cheese

4 slices Havarti cheese

2–3 leaves fresh basil, chopped (optional)

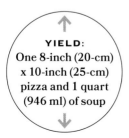

YIELD:
One 8-inch (20-cm)
x 10-inch (25-cm)
pizza and 1 quart
(946 ml) of soup

dry flour remains. Cover and let rest 20 minutes. After 20 minutes, uncover the dough and transfer it to a work surface. Knead for 2 to 3 minutes till mostly smooth. Form the dough into a ball by folding the edges of the dough into the center and repeating the process a few times until the top of the ball is smooth. Pinch the dough ball closed and return it to the bowl. Cover and let rise at room temperature (about 70°F [21°C]) for 6 to 8 hours before making the pizza. If your environment is warmer, transfer the dough to the refrigerator if you see signs of over-fermentation (rapid expansion of the dough, large bubbles). Remove the dough from the refrigerator and let come to room temperature before making the pizza.

3 **To make the pizza:** Preheat your indoor pizza oven with the temperature set to 450°F (230°C).Melt 2 tablespoons (28 g) of the butter in small saucepan over medium heat. Add the clove of garlic and reduce the heat to low. Cook for 5 minutes, stirring often. Remove the clove of garlic and discard or save for another use. Transfer the butter to a small bowl and stir in the garlic powder. Let cool before brushing the pizza dough. When the pizza oven is fully heated, set the heat balance dial (if equipped) to Bottom 5/Top 5.

4 Combine the shredded cheeses in a bowl and set aside until ready to top the pizza. Grease an 8-inch x 10-inch (20-cm x 25-cm) Detroit-style pizza pan with 1 tablespoon (14 g) of butter. Transfer the par-baked Detroit-Style Pizza Dough to the pan. Top with the sliced cheeses, covering the surface of the dough.

5 Uncover the dough ball for the top crust and transfer to a work surface lightly dusted with flour. Flatten the dough ball using your hands. Using a rolling pin dusted with flour, roll out the dough into a roughly 8-inch x 10-inch (20-cm x 25-cm) rectangle. Pick the sheet of dough up with your hands and drape over the sliced

cheese on top of the crust, making sure it covers all the way to the edges. Brush the top of the dough with the garlic butter. Scatter the shredded cheese mixture all over the top and edges of the pizza, covering it completely.

6 Load the pizza into the pizza oven, placing the pan in the center of the baking stone, and bake for 15 minutes, rotating the pan about halfway through the bake. Look for the cheese to melt fully and pull away from the sides of the pan with a golden-brown crust. This pizza has the additional layer of top crust, so make sure the pizza is fully baked.

7 Remove the pan from the oven and let cool for about 1 minute before carefully removing the pizza using a metal spatula. Transfer the pizza to a wire rack to let the crust set for about 1 minute before slicing on a cutting board.

8 Ladle the tomato soup into ramekins. Transfer the sliced pizza to a wire rack nested in a quarter sheet pan to stay crisp while serving. Scatter the chopped basil over the pizza and soup (optional). Enjoy immediately.

Chapter 7
Bar-Style Pan Pizzas

Bar-style pizza is a thin crusted pizza baked till crisp in a shallow round pan. Most commonly found in the bars and taverns of New Jersey, this style of pizza has a super slender crust with the cheese and toppings going all the way to the edge. While thin, the dough is sturdy enough to be generously topped.

With an indoor pizza oven, bar-style pizza is easy. Placing the pan directly on a heated baking stone makes for a nice dough spring as it heats and an even bake. It's straightforward to get a consistent golden-brown bottom without having to resort to multiple baking steps.

While some pizza makers return the pizza to the oven after removing it from the pan, I find this step to be unnecessary when using most indoor pizza ovens. Additionally, any oil left on the bottom of the pizza may cause the oven to smoke heavily and the bottom of the pizza to burn when placed directly on the stone after baking in a pan.

EQUIPMENT AND TOOLS

10-INCH TO 12-INCH (25-CM X 30-CM) ROUND, BAR-STYLE PIZZA PANS

Pans designed for bar-style pizza are typically shallow, seasoned, aluminum pans about ¾-inch to 1½-inch (2 cm to 3.8 cm) deep. The shallow depth and nonstick surface of these pan makes the nearly paper-thin pizzas easy to remove. Some versions even feature a portion of the side of the pan removed so the pizza can be slid on to the baking stone to finish. I find the "nesting" and "cutter" style of pan to be the most versatile.

The recipes are designed for pans in the 10-inch to 12-inch (25-cm to 30-cm) range. Use what fits your oven best. You want a little bit of wiggle room around the pan for the pizza to bake properly.

Alternatively, a cake pan may be used to make bar-style pizza, but the high sides can make the pizza difficult to remove. If using, make sure to grease the pan well to prevent the pizza from sticking.

PAN GRABBER OR OVEN GLOVES

A metal pan grabber or a good set of oven gloves are crucial for easily and safely maneuvering the pans while in the oven as well as removing the hot pizzas from the pan. A pan grabber is especially handy for holding the pan steady while freeing the cheesy, crispy crust from the pan.

METAL SLOTTED TURNER

A flexible, metal slotted turner or fish spatula is perfect for removing bar-style pizza from the pan. The flexible and offset design of these spatulas allows you to sneak under the crust to free any stuck portions of dough without ripping through it.

PIZZA SCREEN AND TRAY FOR SERVING

I like to serve bar-style pizza on a pizza screen nested in a pizza tray to keep it crisp while serving. A little bit of airflow under the warm pizza prevents a steamed, soggy bottom.

BAR-STYLE PAN PIZZA
DOUGH

135 grams filtered water

7 grams kosher salt

1 gram instant dry yeast

210 grams bread flour (Recommended: King Arthur Bread Flour or Central Milling "High Mountain" Flour)

1–2 teaspoons (5–10 ml) avocado oil or other neutral-flavored oil

This bar-style pizza dough is easy to work and bakes up nice and crisp in the pan. A hydration level of around 64 percent makes the dough easy to stretch to form while staying super thin, but it's still high enough to prevent it from drying out during the longer bake. The dough may be proofed in the pan, just make sure not to force the dough immediately to the edges. Let it rest, it should fill it out effortlessly.

1   Pour the filtered water into a large mixing bowl, add the salt, and stir to dissolve completely. Sprinkle the yeast on the surface of the water and let the yeast absorb some of the water for about 1 minute before stirring to dissolve completely. Add the flour.

2   Using your hands, mix the ingredients, stirring and pinching with your fingers till all the ingredients are fully incorporated and no dry flour remains. Do not knead at this point. Cover and let rest at room temperature (about 70°F [21°C]) for 20 to 30 minutes. This rest gives the flour some time to absorb the water and makes the dough easier to knead.

3   After 20 to 30 minutes, uncover the dough and knead for 2 to 3 minutes in the bowl or on a work surface till mostly smooth. Cover and let rest at room temperature for 1 to 2 hours.

4   After 1 to 2 hours, the dough should have risen some and look shiny. Uncover and transfer to a work surface. Lightly knead and fold the dough a few times before shaping into a large ball. Using a bench scraper, divide the dough into 2 equal portions (I use a scale for this). Form each portion into a dough ball by folding the edges of the dough into the center and repeating the process a few times until the tops of the dough balls are smooth. Pinch the
➤

YIELD:
2 pizza dough balls for two 10-inch (25-cm) to 12-inch (30-cm) pizzas

dough balls closed with your fingers. Transfer the dough balls to a lightly oiled dough tray, bowls, or plates. Cover and transfer to the refrigerator to cold ferment for 18 to 72 hours.

5   Alternatively, the dough can be stretched and panned for the cold fermentation process. I find this to be convenient, and it produces great results. Generously oil a 10-inch (25 cm) bar-style pizza pan or 10-inch (25 m) cake pan with olive oil or a neutral flavored oil such as avocado oil. You want to make sure the interior of the pan is fully coated in oil, but there should not be any oil pooled in the pan. Wipe with a paper towel if necessary.

6   Place a dough ball in the center of the pan and press it down into the pan using your palm (a light coat of oil on your hands can help with the stretching process if sticky). Cover and let the dough ball relax for about 15 minutes. Uncover and begin working the dough towards the edges of the pan. Resist the urge to pick the dough up from the pan too much as you may trap air underneath. If the dough is difficult to work, cover and let rest for about 5 minutes before working the dough again. Repeat the process. It often takes about 2 to 3 rest cycles to pan up the dough. Cover and transfer to the refrigerator to cold ferment for 18 to 72 hours.

7   **4 to 6 hours before baking the pizzas:** If you cold fermented your dough as dough balls (not panned), remove them from the refrigerator and transfer to a greased 10-inch (25-cm) bar-style pizza pan or 10-inch (25-cm) cake pan. Let the dough rest in the pan for about 30 minutes before proceeding with the stretching and panning instructions above. If you already panned the dough: **1 to 2 hours before baking the pizza**, remove the panned dough from the refrigerator, keep covered, and let come to room temperature.

BAR-STYLE PAN PIZZA
SAUCE

1 can (28 ounces, or 785 ml) crushed tomatoes

1 tube (4.5 ounces, or 128 g) tomato paste

1 clove garlic, finely minced

½ teaspoon dried oregano

¼ teaspoon garlic powder

¼ teaspoon dried basil

Kosher salt to taste

A smooth and full-flavored pizza sauce that doesn't soak through the dough. This bar-style pizza sauce is amped up with dried herbs and the bite of fresh garlic.

1 Combine the tomatoes, tomato paste, garlic, oregano, garlic powder, and dried basil in a large pot or blender. Blend with an immersion blender or blend on high until completely smooth.

2 Season to taste with kosher salt. The Bar-Style Pizza Sauce can be stored in an airtight container in the refrigerator for up to a week.

YIELD:
About 1 quart
(946 ml)

CLASSIC BAR PIE

2 ½ ounces (71 g) low-moisture whole-milk mozzarella cheese, thickly shredded

2 ½ ounces (71 g) low-moisture part-skim mozzarella cheese, thickly shredded

1 Bar-Style Pan Pizza dough, panned and prepared for topping (see p. 129)

4 ounces (120 ml) Bar-Style Pan Pizza Sauce (see p. 131)

2–3 ounces (56 to 85 g) Monterey Jack cheese, thickly shredded

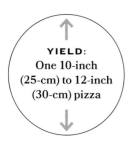

YIELD:
One 10-inch (25-cm) to 12-inch (30-cm) pizza

I stick to the classic flavors found at legendary bar-style pizza places but up the ante with a drool-inducing crispy frico cheese crust. To achieve this, Monterey Jack cheese is added only along the edge of the pan and pizza. It bakes up into a lacey, crispy crust that will have everyone fighting over the last slice.

1 Preheat your indoor pizza oven with the temperature set to 550°F (288°C). When fully heated, set the heat balance dial (if equipped) to Bottom 5/Top 5.

2 Combine the mozzarella cheeses in a bowl and set aside. Ladle the sauce into the center of the pizza and spread it toward the edge leaving a ¼-inch (0.6-cm) of crust between the sauce and the pan. Line the edge of the dough and pan with the Monterey Jack cheese, pushing it up along the sides of the pan to create a crispy frico cheese crust. Scatter the blend of mozzarella cheese evenly over the sauce.

3 Check the temperature of the baking stone. It should be around 550°F to 600°F (288°C to 316°C). Slide the pan onto the center of the baking stone and bake for about 10 minutes, turning a few times as it bakes.

4 When the pizza is fully baked, you should be able to see that the crust has pulled away from the sides of the pan and is golden to dark brown. Remove the pan from the oven and transfer to a wire rack to cool for about 1 minute. Run a metal fish spatula along the edge of the pan to free any bits of crust stuck to the sides of the pan and carefully transfer the pizza to a wire rack to let the crust set for about 1 minute.

5 Transfer the pizza to a wooden peel to slice and slide the pizza onto your serving tray or plate and serve immediately.

GARBAGE BAR PIE

1 Bar-Style Pan Pizza Dough, panned and prepared for topping (see p. 129)

3 ounces (85 g) low-moisture whole-milk mozzarella cheese, thickly shredded

3 ounces (85 g) low-moisture part-skim mozzarella cheese, thickly shredded

5 ounces (150 ml) Bar-Style Pan Pizza Sauce (see p. 131)

3 ounces (85 g) sweet Italian sausage (or homemade Fennel Sausage see p. 73)

1 cup (about 2 ounces [55 g]) shaved white button mushrooms

1 clove garlic, minced

2 ounces (55 g) sliced cupping pepperoni

⅓ cup (38 g) thinly sliced sweet onion

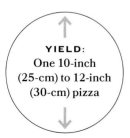

YIELD:
One 10-inch (25-cm) to 12-inch (30-cm) pizza

The signature "kitchen sink" pizza from Patsy's Tavern in Paterson, New Jersey. Legend has it that this pie was born by clearing out the cooler at the end of a shift. An unfortunate name for pie that is anything but garbage.

1 Preheat your indoor pizza oven with the temperature set to 550°F (288°C). When fully heated, set the heat balance dial (if equipped) to Bottom 5/Top 5.

2 Using oiled hands, push and mold the pizza dough all the way up the sides of the pan to create the signature Patsy's Tavern crust. Combine the mozzarella cheeses in a bowl and set aside.

3 Ladle the sauce into the center of the pizza and spread it toward the edge leaving a ¼-inch (0.6-cm) of crust between the sauce and the pan. Spread the cheese evenly over the sauce. Top with the fresh sausage, forming it into marble-size balls. Finish topping the pizza with the shaved mushrooms, garlic, pepperoni, and sliced onion.

4 Check the temperature of the baking stone. It should be around 550°F to 600°F (288°C to 316°C). Slide the pan onto the center of the stone and bake for about 10 minutes, turning a few times. When the pizza is fully baked, you should be able to see that the crust has pulled away from the sides of the pan and is golden to dark brown.

5 Remove the pan from the oven and transfer to a wire rack to cool for about 1 minute. Run a metal fish spatula along the edge of the pan to free any bits of crust stuck to the sides of the pan and carefully transfer the pizza to a wire rack to let the crust set for about 1 minute.

6 Transfer the pizza to a wooden peel to slice and slide the pizza onto your serving tray or plate.

HOT OIL STINGER
BAR PIE

**FOR THE HOT OIL
AND STINGERS:**
1 bottle (16.9 ounces, or
479 ml) extra-virgin olive oil

10 serrano peppers

FOR THE PIZZA:
3 ounces (85 g) low-
moisture whole-milk
mozzarella cheese,
thickly shredded

3 ounces (85 g)
low-moisture part-skim
mozzarella cheese,
thickly shredded

1 Bar-Style Pan Pizza Dough,
panned and prepared for
topping (see p. 129)

4 ounces (120 ml) Bar-Style
Pan Pizza Sauce (see p. 131)

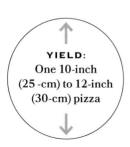

YIELD:
One 10-inch
(25-cm) to 12-inch
(30-cm) pizza

The signature bar pie of the Colony Grill in Stamford, Connecticut. It's topped with hot oil and a "stinger," a whole serrano pepper slowly roasted in oil. It's the crowd favorite for a reason. The signature hot oil topping packs the heat but isn't overwhelming, adding a pleasant *sting* to this epic pizza.

1 **To make the Hot Oil and Stingers:** Empty the bottle of extra-virgin olive oil into a medium-size saucepan and reserve the bottle. Add the serrano peppers and bring to a gentle simmer over low heat. Lower the heat to a simmer and continue cooking, stirring occasionally until the skin of the peppers softens and the peppers are tender. Remove the pan from the heat and let the peppers fully cool in the oil. Remove the peppers and reserve for topping pizzas. Strain the cooled oil through a fine mesh sieve into the reserved bottle for topping pizzas. Infused oils should be stored in the refrigerator. The Hot Oil can be stored in the bottle in the refrigerator for a month or longer. The Stingers (peppers) can also be stored, covered with the Hot Oil, in an airtight container in the refrigerator.

2 **To make the pizza:** Preheat your indoor pizza oven with the temperature set to 550°F (288°C). When fully heated, set the heat balance dial (if equipped) to Bottom 5/Top 5.

3 Combine the whole-milk and part-skim milk mozzarella cheeses in a bowl. Set aside until ready to top the pizza.

4 Ladle the sauce into the center of the pizza and spread it out toward the edge of the pan in a circular motion using the back of the ladle. Leave about a ¼-inch (0.6-cm) buffer of crust between the sauce and edge of the pan. Spread the blend of mozzarella cheese evenly over the sauce and place 1 whole stinger serrano pepper in the center of the pizza.

5 Check the temperature of the baking stone. It should be around 550°F to 600°F (288°C to 316°C) when loading the pizza into the oven. Slide the pan onto the center of the baking stone and bake for about 10 minutes, turning a few times as it bakes.

6 When the pizza is fully baked, you should be able to see that the crust has pulled away from the sides of the pan and is golden to dark brown.

7 Remove the pan from the oven and transfer to a wire rack to cool for about 1 minute. Run a metal fish spatula along the edge of the pan to free any bits of crust stuck to the sides of the pan and carefully transfer the pizza to a wire rack to let the crust set for about 1 minute.

8 Transfer the pizza to a wooden peel to slice and slide the pizza onto your serving tray or plate making sure each piece is still topped with some of the Stinger pepper. Drizzle the entire pizza with 2 tablespoons (28 ml) Hot Oil and serve immediately.

JALAPEÑO POPPER
BAR PIE

2 ounces (55 g) cream cheese, softened

¼ teaspoon garlic powder

Kosher salt to taste

Freshly ground black pepper to taste

2 ounces (55 g) Monterey Jack cheese, thickly shredded

2 ounces (55 g) low-moisture whole-milk mozzarella cheese, thickly shredded

1 Bar-Style Pan Pizza Dough, panned and prepared for topping (see p. 129)

2 ounces (55 g) pepper jack cheese, thickly shredded

2 ounces (55 g) sweet Italian sausage (or homemade Fennel Sausage see p. 73)

1–2 jalapeño peppers, thinly sliced

2 slices thickly sliced uncooked smoked bacon, cut into lardons

2 green onions, thinly sliced, tops reserved

4 ounces (115 g) panko breadcrumbs

Hot Oil (optional, see p. 134)

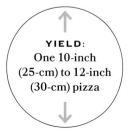

YIELD:
One 10-inch (25-cm) to 12-inch (30-cm) pizza

This jalapeño popper-inspired pizza is a showstopper bar pie that's absolutely delicious. Filled with all the flavors of a crispy bacon-wrapped jalapeño popper, you won't be able to stop eating this one. This is bar pie at its finest!

1 Preheat your indoor pizza oven with the temperature set to 550°F (288°C). When fully heated, set the heat balance dial (if equipped) to Bottom 5/Top 5.

2 Combine the cream cheese and garlic powder in a small bowl, mix to combine, and season to taste with kosher salt and black pepper. Set aside until ready to top the pizza.

3 Combine the Monterey Jack cheese and whole-milk mozzarella cheese in a bowl. Set aside until ready to top the pizza.

4 Top the pizza dough all over with dollops of the garlic cream cheese. Line the area at the edge of the dough and pan with the pepper jack cheese, pushing it up along the sides of the pan. Scatter the shredded cheese mixture all over the top of the pizza. Top with the fresh sausage, forming it into marble-size balls. Wash your hands and continue topping the pizza with the jalapeño slices, bacon, and white parts of the green onion. Sprinkle the topped pizza with the panko breadcrumbs.

5 Check the temperature of the baking stone. It should be around 550°F to 600°F (288°C to 316°C) when loading the pizza into the oven. Slide the pan onto the center of the baking stone and bake for about 10 minutes, turning a few times as it bakes.

6 When the pizza is fully baked, you should be able to see that the crust has pulled away from the sides of the pan and is golden to dark brown.

7 Remove the pan from the oven and transfer to a wire rack to cool for about 1 minute. Run a metal fish spatula along the edge of the pan to free any bits of crust stuck to the sides of the pan and carefully transfer the pizza to a wire rack to let the crust set for about 1 minute.

8 Transfer the pizza to a wooden peel to slice and slide the pizza onto your serving tray or plate. Sprinkle with the sliced green onion tops and a drizzle of Hot Oil (optional). Serve immediately.

CHILI-CRISPED PEPPERONI
BAR PIE

2–3 tablespoons (30 to 45 g) spicy chili crisp, divided

3 ounces (85 g) sliced cupping pepperoni

3 ounces (85 g) low-moisture whole-milk mozzarella cheese, thickly shredded

3 ounces (85 g) low-moisture part-skim mozzarella cheese, thickly shredded

1 Bar-Style Pan Pizza Dough, panned and prepared for topping (see p. 129)

4 ounces (120 ml) Bar-Style Pan Pizza Sauce (see p. 131)

1 tablespoon Pickled Shallots, drained (see p. 88)

Small handful fresh basil

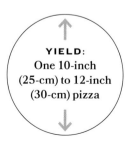

YIELD:
One 10-inch (25-cm) to 12-inch (30-cm) pizza

Cupping pepperoni gets sliced and filled with spicy, umami rich chili crisp before topping the pizza. This pizza packs a punch, but Pickled Shallots and post-bake fresh basil helps to finish it off fresh. Using a pan for this pizza recipe is key. It keeps the oil in the chili crisp from spilling on to the oven deck, so instead the pizza is "fried" in the oil, adding another dimension of flavor. This pizza is deeply delicious.

1 Preheat your indoor pizza oven with the temperature set to 550°F (288°C). When fully heated, set the heat balance dial (if equipped) to Bottom 5/Top 5.

2 Combine 2 tablespoons (30 g) chili crisp with the cupping pepperoni in a bowl. Toss well to fully coat all the pepperoni slices. Set aside until ready to top the pizza.

3 Combine the whole-milk and part-skim milk mozzarella cheeses in a bowl. Set aside until ready to top the pizza.

4 Ladle the sauce into the center of the pizza crust and spread it out toward the edge of the pan in a circular motion using the back of the ladle. Leave about a ¼-inch (0.6-cm) buffer of crust between the sauce and edge of the pan. Scatter the blend of mozzarella cheese evenly over the sauce all the way to edge of the pan. Cover the cheese in the chili-crisped pepperoni and scatter the Pickled Shallots all over the top of the pizza.

5 Check the temperature of the baking stone. It should be around 550°F to 600°F (288°C to 316°C) when loading the pizza into the oven. Slide the pan onto the center of the baking stone and bake for about 10 minutes, turning a few times as it bakes.

6 When the pizza is fully baked, you should be able to see that the crust has pulled away from the sides of the pan and is golden to dark brown. The pepperoni should be cupped and crisped up in some places.

7 Remove the pan from the oven and transfer to a wire rack to cool for about 1 minute. Run a metal fish spatula along the edge of the pan to free any bits of crust stuck to the sides of the pan and carefully transfer the pizza to a wire rack to let the crust set for about 1 minute.

8 Transfer the pizza to a wooden peel to slice and slide the pizza onto your serving tray. Tear the basil directly on to the pizza and drizzle with more chili crisp (optional). Serve immediately.

Chapter 8
Handhelds and Desserts

The clean and even heat of an indoor pizza oven is perfect for baking a wide variety of delicious goodies beyond pizza. From bread to brownies, most recipes that can be baked in a standard home oven can be baked with excellent results in an electric pizza oven.

This chapter is full of some of my favorite "pizza adjacent" recipes that I'll fire up my oven for. Handheld heavy hitters like empanadas and mini calzones excel in the oven. Make the Detroit-Style Brownie Pizza—it's encased in a chocolate chip cookie crust that will have people battling for the corner slice.

MINI CALZONE AND EMPANADA
DOUGH

225 grams filtered water

11 grams kosher salt

1 gram instant dry yeast (room temperature more than 70°F) or 2 grams instant dry yeast (room temperature less than 70°F)

7 grams avocado oil or other neutral oil, plus more as needed

375 grams all-purpose flour

YIELD:
12 dough balls

My dough for epic, handheld deliciousness. The recipe can be used for both the mini calzone and empanada dough recipes. I use all-purpose flour here for a more tender crust. You don't want these to be too chewy. A longer cold proofing time can make for an even better texture.

1 **At least 24 hours before baking:** Pour the filtered water into a large mixing bowl, add the salt, and stir to dissolve completely. Sprinkle the yeast on the surface of the water and let the yeast absorb some of the water for about 1 minute before stirring to dissolve completely. Pour in the oil and add the flour.

2 Using your hands, mix the ingredients, stirring and pinching with your fingers till all the ingredients are fully incorporated and no dry flour remains and the oil is well distributed. Do not knead at this point. Cover and let rest at room temperature (about 70°F [21°C]) for 20 to 30 minutes.

3 After the rest, uncover the dough and knead for 2 to 3 minutes directly in the bowl or on a work surface till mostly smooth. Cover and transfer to the refrigerator for at least 12 hours or up to 72 hours.

4 **About 6 to 8 hours before baking:** Remove the bowl of dough from the refrigerator and let rest at room temperature (about 70°F [21°C]) for about 30 minutes.

5 Transfer the dough to a work surface and divide it into 12 equal portions using a bench scraper.

6 Lightly coat a dough tray or sheet pan with oil. Set aside.

7 Form each portion into a dough ball by folding the edges of the dough into the center and repeating the process a few times until the tops of the dough balls are smooth. Pinch the dough balls closed with your fingers and place on your work surface. Give each dough ball a couple spins with your hands to smooth out the bottom a bit. Transfer the dough balls to the dough tray or sheet pan. Lightly brush the dough balls with oil and cover.

8 Let proof at room temperature (about 70°F [21°C]) for at least 1 to 2 hours before proceeding with shaping and filling.

CRISPY MORTADELLA AND PROVOLONE
MINI CALZONES

1 tablespoon (15 ml) extra-virgin olive oil

8 ounces (225 g) mortadella, cut into small cubes

12 Mini Calzone and Empanada Dough balls (see p. 142)

All-purpose flour as needed

6 ounces (170 g) provolone cheese, thickly shredded

Rice flour as needed

1 egg, beaten

YIELD:
12 mini calzones

The simple, classic combination of mortadella and provolone cheese is a popular filling for *panzerotto*, a small fried calzone popular in central and southern Italy. Instead of the traditional thin slices, I dice the mortadella into small cubes and cook till crisp before filling. As the fat in the mortadella renders in the pan, the cubes crisp into golden brown morsels of deliciousness, so good you could just serve them on their own. Ask the deli counter to cut you a large chunk or very thick slices to cube yourself.

1 Heat the olive oil in a skillet over medium heat. Add the mortadella and cook, stirring often till golden brown and crispy. Remove the crispy mortadella from the pan using a slotted spoon and transfer to a paper towel–lined plate to cool. Let cool to room temperature before filling the mini calzones.

2 To stretch the mini calzones, dust a work surface (about 2 feet x 2 feet [61 cm x 61 cm]) with flour. Transfer a dough ball to the floured surface. Lightly dust the top of the dough ball with flour and press down on the top of the ball with the palm of your hand to flatten. Flip the dough and push out into a circle. Dust a wooden rolling pin with flour and roll the dough out into a 5-inch (13 cm) circle. Repeat with the remaining dough balls. If the stretched dough is sticking to your work surface, dust with additional flour.

3 Heat your pizza oven with the temperature set to 550°F (288°C).

4 While the oven is heating, fill the mini calzones. Begin by placing a small amount of shredded cheese in the center of each circle of stretched dough. Push the cheese into the dough using your hands and top with a few pieces of crispy mortadella and another small amount of shredded cheese. Push the mixture gently into

the dough and fold the dough closed. Using the tines of a fork, seal the dough closed by pushing the tines into the rim of the dough and pulling away to seal. Dip the fork in a small amount of flour to prevent sticking. Transfer to a parchment-lined sheet pan dusted with rice flour. Repeat the final filling and sealing process with the remaining mini calzone dough.

5 Once the oven is fully heated, set the heat control setting to Bottom 4/Top 6 (if equipped).

6 Brush the tops of each of the mini calzones with the beaten egg using a pastry brush.

7 Slide 4 to 6 mini calzones into oven. I find a turning peel works great for this. Bake, turning occasionally, till puffed and very golden brown, about 8 minutes. Remove and let cool briefly on a wire rack before serving.

PANCETTA, WILD ARUGULA, AND FONTINA
MINI CALZONES

12 Mini Calzone and
Empanada Dough balls
(see p. 142)

All-purpose flour as needed

8 ounces (225 g) fontina
cheese, thickly shredded

1 clove garlic, minced

4 ounces (115 g) diced
pancetta cooked till just
crisp, cooled

3 cups (60 g) wild arugula

Rice flour as needed

1 egg, beaten

YIELD:
12 mini
calzones

Wild arugula cuts through the bacon-like richness of the pancetta and fontina cheese for a pocket packed full of flavors and textures. It's a simple combination that tastes bigger than it is.

1 To stretch the mini calzones, dust a work surface (about 2 feet x 2 feet [61 cm x 61 cm]) with flour. Transfer a dough ball to the floured surface. Lightly dust the top of the dough ball with flour and press down on the top of the ball with the palm of your hand to flatten. Flip the dough and push out into a circle. Dust a wooden rolling pin with flour and roll the dough out into a 5-inch (13 cm) circle. Repeat with the remaining dough balls. If the stretched dough is sticking to your work surface, dust with additional flour.

2 Heat your pizza oven with the temperature set to 550°F (288°C).

3 While the oven is heating, fill the mini calzones. Begin by placing a small amount of shredded cheese in the center of each circle of stretched dough. Push the cheese into the dough using your hands and top with a pinch of minced garlic followed by a few pieces of diced pancetta. Grab a small handful of arugula and crumple into a tight ball using your hand. Place the ball in the center of the toppings and fold over to close. Be sure to tuck all the toppings inside (do not overfill!). Using the tines of a fork, seal the dough closed by pushing the tines into the rim of the dough and pulling away to seal. Dip the fork in a small amount of flour to prevent sticking. Transfer to a parchment-lined sheet pan dusted with rice flour. Repeat the final filling and sealing process with the remaining mini calzone dough.

4 Once the oven is fully heated, set the heat control setting to Bottom 4/Top 6 (if equipped).

5 Brush the tops of each of the mini calzones with the beaten egg using a pastry brush.

6 Slide 4 to 6 mini calzones into oven. I find a turning peel works great for this. Bake, turning occasionally, till puffed and very golden brown, about 8 minutes. Remove and let cool briefly on a wire rack before serving.

SPICY BEEF, CHEESE, AND SALSA FRESCA
EMPANADAS

||||||||||||||||||||||||||||||||||||||||||||||||||

FOR THE SPICY BEEF FILLING:

1 pound (455 g) ground beef

1 teaspoon chili powder

1 teaspoon dried Mexican oregano

½ teaspoon ground cumin

½ teaspoon garlic powder

½ teaspoon onion powder

Kosher salt to taste

Freshly ground black pepper to taste

½ cup (80 g) finely diced yellow onion

2 cloves garlic, minced

1 jalapeño pepper, minced

2 tablespoons (32 g) tomato paste

FOR THE EMPANADAS:

12 Mini Calzone and Empanada Dough balls (p. 142)

All-purpose flour as needed

8 ounces (225 g) queso Oaxaca, thickly shredded

12 ounces (340 g) fresh pico de gallo, drained of excess liquid

Rice flour as needed

1 egg, beaten

F illed with seasoned ground beef, melty Oaxaca cheese, and fresh salsa, these empanadas just might flash you back to memories of discontinued fast-food items, but elevated of course. Make sure to use a freshly made salsa for this one. The flavor and texture of the fresh tomatoes are key here as they tend to get lost in jarred versions.

1 **To make the Spicy Beef Filling:** Heat a large skillet over medium-high heat and add the ground beef. Break up any large chunks of beef (I find a potato masher to be excellent for this) and add the dried spices. Cook till browned, about 5 minutes. Add the onion, garlic, and jalapeño and cook over medium-high heat till softened, 2 to 3 minutes. Add the tomato paste and stir well. Continue cooking over medium-high heat for 1 to 2 minutes till reduced. Transfer the cooked filling to a bowl to let cool fully before using. The Spicy Beef Filling can be stored in an airtight container in the refrigerator for 3 to 4 days.

2 **To make the empanadas:** To stretch the empanadas, dust a work surface (about 2 feet x 2 feet [61 cm x 62 cm]) with flour. Transfer a dough ball to the floured surface. Lightly dust the top of the dough ball with flour and press down on the top of the ball with the palm of your hand to flatten. Flip the dough and push out into a circle. Dust a wooden rolling pin with flour and roll the dough out into a 5-inch (13 cm) circle. Repeat with the remaining dough balls. If the stretched dough is sticking to your work surface, dust with additional flour.

3 Heat your pizza oven with the temperature set to 550°F (288°C).
➤➤

YIELD:
12 empanadas

4 While the oven is heating, fill the empanadas. Begin by placing a small amount of shredded cheese in the center of each circle of stretched dough. Push the cheese into the dough using your hands and top with a spoonful of the Spicy Beef Filling and a spoonful of pico de gallo. Top with a pinch of shredded cheese and fold closed. Using the tines of a fork, seal the dough closed by pushing the tines into the rim of the dough and pulling away to seal. Dip the fork in a small amount of flour to prevent sticking. Transfer to a parchment-lined sheet pan dusted with rice flour. Repeat the final filling and sealing process with the dough.

5 Once the oven is fully heated, set the heat control setting to Bottom4/Top 6 (if equipped).

6 Brush the tops of each of the empanadas with the beaten egg using a pastry brush.

7 Slide 4 to 6 empanadas into oven. I find a turning peel works great for this. Bake, turning occasionally, till puffed and very golden brown, about 8 minutes. Remove and let cool briefly on a wire rack before serving.

SPINACH, GOAT CHEESE, QUINOA, AND PIQUILLO PEPPER
EMPANADAS

|||||||||||||||||||||||||||||||||||||

FOR THE QUINOA:

7 ounces (207 grams) filtered water

½ cup (87 g) red quinoa, rinsed

FOR THE FILLING:

3 cups (90 g) baby spinach

4 ounces (115 g) fresh goat cheese, crumbled

½ cup (130 g) diced piquillo peppers (about 4–5 whole peppers)

1 small lemon, juice and zest

1 shallot, minced

Kosher salt to taste

Freshly ground black pepper to taste

FOR THE EMPANADAS:

12 Mini Calzone and Empanada Dough balls (p. 142)

All-purpose flour as needed

Rice flour as needed

1 egg, beaten

YIELD:
12 empanadas

Tangy goat cheese and nutty quinoa pair up perfectly with sweet piquillo peppers and spinach in this veggie empanada.

1 **To make the quinoa:** Pour the water into a small pot and add the quinoa. Bring to a boil over high heat, cover, and reduce the heat to a simmer. Cook, covered, for 15 minutes. Remove the pot from the heat and let sit covered for 10 minutes. Fluff with a fork. Let cool before mixing with the remaining filling ingredients.

2 **To make the filling:** Combine the cooked quinoa (about 2 cups [370 g]), baby spinach, goat cheese, piquillo peppers, and shallot in large bowl and mix well. The mixing process should wilt the spinach slightly, making the empanadas easier to fill. Season to taste with kosher salt and black pepper.

3 **To stretch the empanadas,** dust a work surface (about 2 feet x 2 feet [61 cm x 61 cm]) with flour. Transfer a dough ball to the floured surface. Lightly dust the top of the dough ball with flour and press down on the top of the ball with the palm of your hand to flatten. Flip the dough and push out into a circle. Dust a wooden rolling pin with flour and roll the dough out into a 5-inch (13 cm) circle. Repeat with the remaining dough balls. If the stretched dough is sticking to your work surface, dust with additional flour.

4 Heat your pizza oven with the temperature set to 550°F (288°C). ➥

5 While the oven is heating, fill the empanadas. Place a spoonful of the filling in the center of the dough and fold closed. Using the tines of a fork, seal the dough closed by pushing the tines into the rim of the dough and pulling away to seal. Dip the fork in a small amount of flour to prevent sticking. Transfer to a parchment-lined sheet pan dusted with rice flour. Repeat the final filling and sealing process with the dough.

6 Once the oven is fully heated, set the heat control setting to Bottom4/Top 6 (if equipped).

7 Brush the tops of each of the empanadas with the beaten egg using a pastry brush.

8 Slide 4 to 6 empanadas into oven. I find a turning peel works great for this. Bake, turning occasionally, till puffed and very golden brown, about 8 minutes. Remove and let cool briefly on a wire rack before serving.

DETROIT-STYLE BROWNIE PIZZA
WITH CHOCOLATE CHIP COOKIE CRUST

FOR THE CHOCOLATE CHIP COOKIE CRUST:

1 box (16.75 ounces, or 474 g) Ghirardelli Dark Chocolate Chip Premium Mix

1 egg

1 stick (8 tablespoons, or 112 g) unsalted butter or 4 ounces (115 g) ghee, softened

FOR THE BROWNIE PIZZA:

¼ cup (60 ml) water or cold brew coffee

½ cup (120 ml) avocado oil or other neutral oil

1 egg

1 box (20 ounces, or 567 g) Ghirardelli Dark Chocolate Brownie Mix

1 tablespoon (14 g) unsalted butter, for greasing the pan

YIELD:
About 24 slices

When I was dreaming this one up, I knew it would be good, but I didn't realize just how ridiculously delicious it would be, especially baked as a "pizza."

I'm typically not one for using packaged baking mixes, but for this recipe, I make an exception. The mix keeps it really easy, and the results will leave you with trouble keeping the milk stocked—it's that good. If you're feeling the vibe to go "all-scratch," you can substitute your favorite homemade brownie and/or chocolate chip cookie recipe here.

1 **To make the Chocolate Chip Cookie Crust** (at least 1 hour before baking)**:** Combine the chocolate chip cookie mix, egg, and softened butter in a bowl. Stir and knead with your hands until all the ingredients are fully incorporated. Cover and transfer to the refrigerator to chill for 1 to 3 hours.

2 **To make the Brownie Pizza:** Preheat your indoor pizza oven with the temperature set to 300°F (150°C). When the pizza oven is fully heated, set the heat balance dial (if equipped) to Bottom 5/Top 5.

3 Combine the water or coffee, avocado oil, and egg in a bowl. Add the brownie mix and stir until all the ingredients are fully incorporated. Set aside.

4 Grease an 8-inch x 10-inch (20-cm to 25-cm) Detroit-style pizza pan with butter.

5 Remove the chocolate chip cookie dough from the refrigerator and uncover. Scoop 12 teaspoon-size (5 ml) balls of dough and reserve on a piece of parchment paper or plate. Apply the remaining cookie dough in an even layer to the interior edge of the pan, going all the way up the sides of the pan. Set aside. ➤➤

6 Pour the brownie mix into the center of the pan and spread evenly all the way up to the cookie crust. Top the brownie batter with the 12 reserved balls of cookie dough in 2 rows of 6.

7 Slide the pan into the center of the baking stone and bake 45 minutes to 1 hour, rotating the pan a few times as it bakes. Baking times may vary significantly. Keep an eye on it around the 45-minute mark. When fully baked, the brownie batter should be set and not move around when you shake the pan.

8 Remove the pan from the oven and let cool on a wire rack, at least 1 hour, before removing from the pan with a metal spatula. Slice and serve immediately, preferably still slightly warm with a scoop of vanilla ice cream.

ACKNOWLEDGMENTS

I've stopped wondering when I'll get sick of pizza. This answer is never. The journey to delicious pizza is never dull and it's never-ending. Just when I think I've tasted my ideal slice, a new contender presents itself. It's the world's greatest food and I love sharing it with you. Pizza changed my life and I couldn't be more grateful for the change.

Thank you especially to all my family. Pizza became your lifestyle too and I'm thankful you've embraced it. Mom and Dad, thank you for all your love and support. Kristin, for eating pizza eight times and week and for always being my number one taste tester. Violet, for being my biggest fan and never letting me forget the importance of just cheese and sauce. Special thanks to Grandpa Matt for all the hours making sure matters more important than pizza were well taken care of.

Big thanks to the team at Harvard Common Press at Quarto. Especially Dan Rosenberg, Editorial Director, thank you for your continued support in making pizza cookbooks essential for every food lovers' library. Gabrielle Bethancourt-Hughes, Editorial Project Manager, gracious thanks for all your time working through the important details to make sure this cookbook gets it right and inspires people to make amazing pizza.

The possibility of working with the amazing photographer and food stylist team, Andrew and Carrie Purcell, was one element of this project I was most looking forward to. I'm so happy we were able to make it happen; your skills and vision make everything look so delicious. Photo shoots filled with good vibes and food you can't stop eating need to be a regular thing. Thank you so much for the beautiful images and fun times making them.

Most of all, many thanks to all the pizza lovers out there that keep me inspired to continue creating and eating delicious pizza. I can't wait to share my next slice with you.

ABOUT THE AUTHOR

After successfully sharing techniques and recipes in the *Epic Outdoor Pizza Oven Cookbook*, author, Jonathon Schuhrke, brings his pizza passionate lifestyle indoors. Schuhrke started his pizza journey day-dreaming about pizza, while working as a geographer. He ditched the office life and put his hands on the dough taking a job as a pizza maker at a world-renowned pizzeria. Since then, he has combined his science background, restaurant kitchen experience, and true passion to share the secrets to amazing homemade pizza on his Santa Barbara Baker media channels. "Making pizzas is what my hands want to do. Thinking about pizza is what my mind wants to do. Eating pizza is what my mouth wants to do. The love is real," he writes. Celebrated by the press and respected within the pizza community, Schuhrke is a creative recipe developer and expert on home pizza making. He shares his kitchen skills, wisdom and good vibes on his website SantaBarbaraBaker.com and on his Instagram and YouTube channels. He combines years of experience as a chef with a knack for ingredient paring to provide a wealth of inventive recipes and time-tested techniques for making every kind of pizza from niche, regional favorites to universal classics. He lives, makes, and eats pizza in Santa Barbara, California.

Index